English Code 6

Student's Book

Contents

Unit	Unit aims	Vocabulary and Phonics	Values
Welcome! pp. 4–9	How can I talk about my schedule? • Use school day words. • Use *like*.	**School words:** assembly, bell's ringing, cafeteria, detention, gym, hallway, locker, lunch box, portable classroom, recess, schedule, stand in line, study hall	Be welcoming.
1 In the news pp. 10–23	How can I make a video news report? • Use social media and news words. • Talk about what others have said. • Talk about what others have asked. • Write a podcast.	**Social media:** blog, caption, cyberbullying, headline, interview, news article, online, report, reporter, sharing, sources, upload, vlog **Phonics:** vlog, lot, watch, on, club, fun, come, good, put cyberbullying	Fact checking.
2 Inspirational people pp. 24–37	How can I make a book about inspirational people? • Use words to describe people and their jobs. • Use relative clauses. • Talk about past habits and states. • Write a biography.	**Jobs:** author, campaigner, charity worker, lawyer, researcher, volunteer **Adjectives:** brave, compassionate, determined, generous, inspirational, intelligent **Phonics:** beach, clean, eat, read, sea feathers, head, healthy, read, wealthy	Value yourself.
Checkpoint	Review Units 1–2	pp. 38–39	
Culture	Sweden	pp. 40–41	
3 Let's earn money! pp. 42–55	How can I make an advertisement for my business? • Use money words. • Talk about obligation and advice. • Ask for help. • Write an advertisement.	**Business words:** advertisement, cash, earn, invent, price, product, save, sell, spend **Phonics:** yellow, gold, blow, boat, float interview, few blue, new, shoes	Fund our school.
4 Food for the future! pp. 56–69	How can I create a sustainable farm for the future? • Use food and farming words. • Talk about the future. • Talk about future possibilities. • Write about an event in a newsletter.	**Food:** carbohydrate, dairy, fats, fiber, minerals, protein, vitamins **Farming:** agriculture, intensive farming, organic farming, pesticides, pollinators, sustainable farming **Phonics:** August, caught, four, saw, thought blue, drew, flew, flute, June, true	Food sustainability.
Checkpoint	Review Units 3–4	pp. 70–71	
Culture	Kenya	pp. 72–73	
5 The ancient world pp. 74–87	How can I make an audio tour guide about the past? • Use words to describe ancient Egypt • Use the Past Passive. • Ask questions in the Past Passive. • Write a fact file.	**Ancient Egypt:** archeologist, burial place, coffin, digging, hieroglyphics, hole, mummy, papyrus, pyramid, treasure **Phonics:** work, word where, treasure, there	Our history.
6 On the move! pp. 88–101	How can I help exchange students in my town? • Use airport words. • Use the Present Perfect Progressive. • Talk about recent events. • Write a feedback form.	**Airport:** arrivals, baggage, check-in, departure gate, emigrating, land, language exchange, passport, security, take off, terminal **Phonics:** our, hours, flower, tower fire, tire, hire	Care for our world.
Checkpoint	Review Units 5–6	pp. 102–103	
Culture	The United Kingdom	pp. 104–105	
7 I hate it when … pp. 106–119	How can I design a board game about fears? • Use words to describe challenging situations. • Use the Present Perfect and Simple Past. • Talk about giving a presentation. • Write a dialog.	**Challenging situations:** called your teacher "Mom", dropped your phone, forgotten your words, got lost in a maze, looked down from the top of a skyscraper, overslept and missed class, slept alone in the dark, slipped on a banana skin, texted the wrong person, turned off the internet **Phonics:** wrap, wrist thumb, climbing know, knot bright, night	Challenge yourself.
8 My amazing city pp. 120–133	How can I create a project to change my city? • Use town and city words. • Use the second conditional. • Ask for and give directions. • Writing instructions.	**City words:** city hall, crosswalk, factory, office building, overpass, sidewalk, skyscraper, stadium, statue, tunnel, university **Phonics:** a European city, a hospital, a one-way street, a university, an elegant city, an hour, an office building, an underground train	Choose your environment.
Checkpoint	Review Units 7–8	pp. 134–135	
Culture	U.S.A.	pp. 136–137	

Writing	Structures		STEAM	Project and Review
	Language lab What's he **like**? He's shy and quiet. What does he **like**? He likes science. What does he **look like**? He's tall and has short hair.			
Write a podcast.	**Language lab** He **said** that he **watch**ed the news. They **said** that they **had** a funny news story to tell. I **said** that I **was** interested in the news.	**Communication** I asked him if he had any brothers or sisters. She asked me what time I got up in the morning.	**Science:** Freezing liquids and solids **Experiment:** What happens when you freeze different materials?	Make a video news report.
Write a biography.	**Language lab** She's the woman **who** works as a charity worker. That's the lion **that** he rescued. This is **where** the politician lived.	**Communication** I **used to** live in Texas. She **didn't use to** go to school. **Did you use to** study English?	**Science:** Mold and bacteria **Experiment:** Which condition does mold grow best in?	Make a class book of inspirational people.
Write an advertisement.	**Language lab** You **should** listen to the rules. You **have to** pay with cash. You **don't have to** buy all the cookies. You **must** stand in line.	**Communication** Would you do me a favor and open the door, please? Could we borrow a pencil, please?	**Math:** Spending and earning money **Experiment:** Calculating profit and loss	Make a video advertisement for your business.
Write about an event in a newsletter.	**Language lab** It **will** rain tomorrow. It's **going to** be delicious. I'm visiting an organic farm on Saturday.	**Communication** We **might** grow food in laboratories in the future. He's a vegan so he **might not** eat anything on the menu.	**Science:** Food chains **Experiment:** How does energy pass through an ocean food chain?	Create a 3D plan of a sustainable farm for the future.
Write a fact file.	**Language lab** My name **was written** in hieroglyphics. The pyramids **were visited** by tourist.	**Communication** Why was it built? Was it moved? Yes, it was.	**Engineering:** How the pyramids were built **Experiment:** How do different surfaces affect friction?	Make an audio tour guide about the past.
Give feedback.	**Language lab** I've **been waiting** in line at check-in for hours! They **haven't been staying** with a host family.	**Communication** Have you arrived yet? Yes, we've just arrived here. Have you checked in already?	**Technology:** Iris recognition **Experiment:** Can I recognize my classmates just from their eyes?	Create a welcome pack to help exchange students settle in your town.
Write a dialog.	**Language lab** **Have you ever taken** a ride in a helicopter? Yes, I **have**. **When did you do** that? I **went** in a helicopter last summer.	**Communication** Introduce the topic. Use personal experiences. Order your points. End the presentation.	**Science:** What happens when we feel fear? **Experiment:** Measuring heart rate	Design and make a board game about fears.
Write instructions.	**Language lab** **If I were** a millionaire, **I'd** buy a huge apartment in a skyscraper. She **wouldn't** use the crosswalk **if there was** an overpass.	**Communication** How do I get to the stadium? I'd go across the park. Go along this street.	**Design:** Water features **Experiment:** Create a water pump!	Create a project to change your city.

Welcome!

How can I talk about my school schedule?

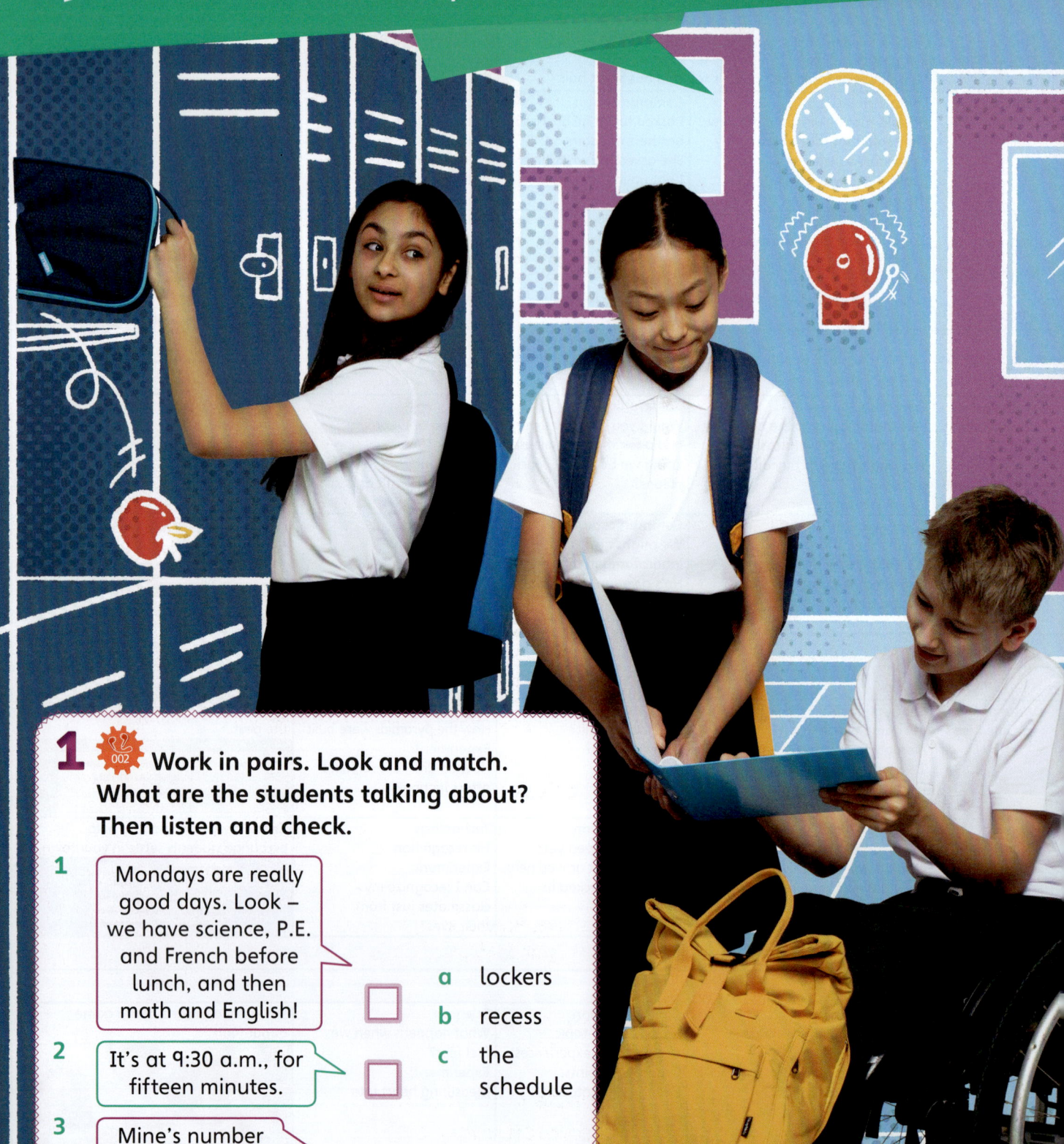

1 Work in pairs. Look and match. What are the students talking about? Then listen and check.

1. Mondays are really good days. Look – we have science, P.E. and French before lunch, and then math and English!

2. It's at 9:30 a.m., for fifteen minutes.

3. Mine's number 132. What number is yours?

a lockers
b recess
c the schedule

2 Look at the schedule. Read the sentences and circle T (True) or F (False).

	MONDAY	TUESDAY	WEDNESDAY	THURSDAY	FRIDAY
8:30–9:30	science	math	science	math	science
9:30–9:45	RECESS				
9:45–10:15	P.E.	music	art	French	math
10:15–11:15	French	French	technology	French	math
11:15–12:15	LUNCH				
12:15–12:45	math	English	math	English	P.E.
12:45–1:45	math	English	math	English	French
1:45–2:00	RECESS				
2:00–3:00	English	science	English	science	English

1 We have technology twice a week. T / F
2 We have P.E. at the beginning and end of the week. T / F
3 Afternoon recess is longer than morning recess. T / F
4 The lunch break is an hour long. T / F

3 Work in pairs. Ask and answer.

1 What time is recess? What do you do then?
2 What time is lunch? Where do you have lunch?
3 Look at your schedule. What's your favorite day and class?

> What time is recess?

> Morning recess is at 9:30 a.m. Afternoon recess is at 1:45 p.m.

4 Make and decorate a notebook cover. You can use colored paper or cloth – or recycled objects!

The school day
VOCABULARY

I will learn words to talk about the school day.

1 Match the sentences with the photos.

a Chatting to my friends at **recess**.

b Here we are in the **cafeteria**. What's in my **lunch box** today?

c The **bell's ringing**! It's time to **stand in line**.

d Our English class is in a **portable classroom** this term!

e Oh, no. Jose has to go to **study hall** for **detention**!

f This is my **locker**! It's my lucky number, too.

g Hey! No running in the **hallway**!

h Every Friday we have **assembly** in the **gym**.

i This is my **schedule**. It's in my homework planner.

2 Can you figure out the puzzle? Where are Chen, Alicia, and Yildiz? What are they doing there?

CODE CRACKER

- Chen is in the portable classroom.
- The person that is outside the cafeteria is standing in line.
- Alicia isn't standing in line.
- The person that is in study hall is doing homework.

	in the portable classroom	in study hall	outside the cafeteria	in an English class	doing homework	standing in line
Chen	✓	✗	✗			
Alicia						
Yildiz						

Language lab

GRAMMAR: *LIKE*

I will learn the different uses of **like**.

1 Write the words below under the correct headings. Add more words to each.

curly hair   English   friendly   math
P.E.   quiet   science   short hair
shy   sporty   tall   wears glasses

be like / like / look like

What **is** he / she **like**? = a question about someone's personality

What **does** he / she **like**? = a question about someone's likes / dislikes

What **does** he / she **look like**? = a question about someone's appearance

Physical appearance	Personality	School subjects

2 Match the questions to the answers.

1 What does he look like?
2 What does she like?
3 What does she look like?
4 What is he like?
5 What does he like?
6 What is she like?

a He likes science and computer coding.
b She's shy and quiet.
c He's tall and has short, curly, black hair.
d She likes English and art.
e She's short and has long, straight, red hair.
f He's really friendly.

3 Play *Guess Who It Is* with a partner.

I'm thinking of a girl.

What is she like?

What does she like?

seven 7

Story lab
READING

I will read a comedy story.

1 Read the story quickly and answer. Who is Samira? Check ✓.

a The school principal ☐
b A Welcome Buddy ☐
c The new kid at school ☐

The wrong Riley

"Riley, there's a letter from Summertown Junior High here for you," yelled Mom. My stomach turned upside down. It was my first day of term at a new school on Monday and I was feeling a little nervous.

It was my Grade 6 schedule and a letter from the principal. Then something else caught my eye. "Hey, look – a message from my Welcome Buddy! She's called Samira."

"What's she like?" asked Mom.

"She seems really friendly. She likes science and math, but she doesn't like P.E. Oh, look, here's a photo."

"She sounds a lot like you! What does she look like?" asked Mom.

"She's got long, dark hair and glasses. I'll buy her a little gift for being my Welcome Buddy."

I arrived for my first day of school clutching a science book as a gift for Samira. I saw her in a group of Welcome Buddies standing near the lockers. She didn't look exactly like she did in the photo – her hair was short and she wasn't wearing glasses – but it was definitely her.

"Hi, I'm Riley – you're my Welcome Buddy!" I said. "This is for you." I handed her my gift. She didn't look very happy.

"Hi Riley. Uh, thanks for the book," she answered. "I guess you want to see the gym and the sports field first. I'm so excited that you were the P.E. captain in your last school. I love P.E. – I'm the P.E. captain here."

"Oh," I said, a little confused. "I'd rather see the science laboratory first."

"Really?!" exclaimed Samira. "You like science?!"

"Yes," I said. "I thought you did, too …"

"Hmmmm, not so much," she replied.

This was strange! Why did Samira lie in her Welcome Buddy letter? And why did she think I was P.E. captain?

We walked down the hallway into the science lab and suddenly there were two Samiras – my Samira and her double with long hair and glasses, showing a confused-looking girl in sportswear around the lab.

"Look – it's my twin," said my Samira. "Hey Samira, this is Riley. He likes science like you."

"Hi Shemina! My Welcome Buddy is called Riley, too! And she likes P.E. like you!" said the real Samira.

"I think we got the wrong Riley!" laughed Samira and Shemina, identically.

2 Read the story again. Answer.

1 What does Riley like?

2 What does Riley's Welcome Buddy look like in her photo?

3 What does she look like when he meets her?

4 What does Riley want to see first?

5 Does Shemina like science?

6 Which Riley, the girl or the boy, likes P.E.?

3 Rewrite the story from the point of view of the girl Riley and the real Samira. Act out the story in groups.

Values Be welcoming.

4 Work in pairs and discuss.

1 Can you remember your first day at school? How did you feel?

2 What type of personality do you think the Welcome Buddies need?

3 Would you be a good Welcome Buddy? Why or why not?

nine 9

1 In the news

How can I make a video news report?

1 Look and discuss. How do you find out about the news? What kind of news are you most interested in?

SKATEBOARDING CHAMPION

Sky Brown Skateboard Champion

HUGE SNOWSTORM HITS THE USA

2 Identify the following in the photo.

1. a headline
2. a reporter
3. an article
4. online news

HUGE SNOWSTOR HITS THE

3 Which news report would you like to find out more about? Write three questions to ask about it.

_____
_____
_____

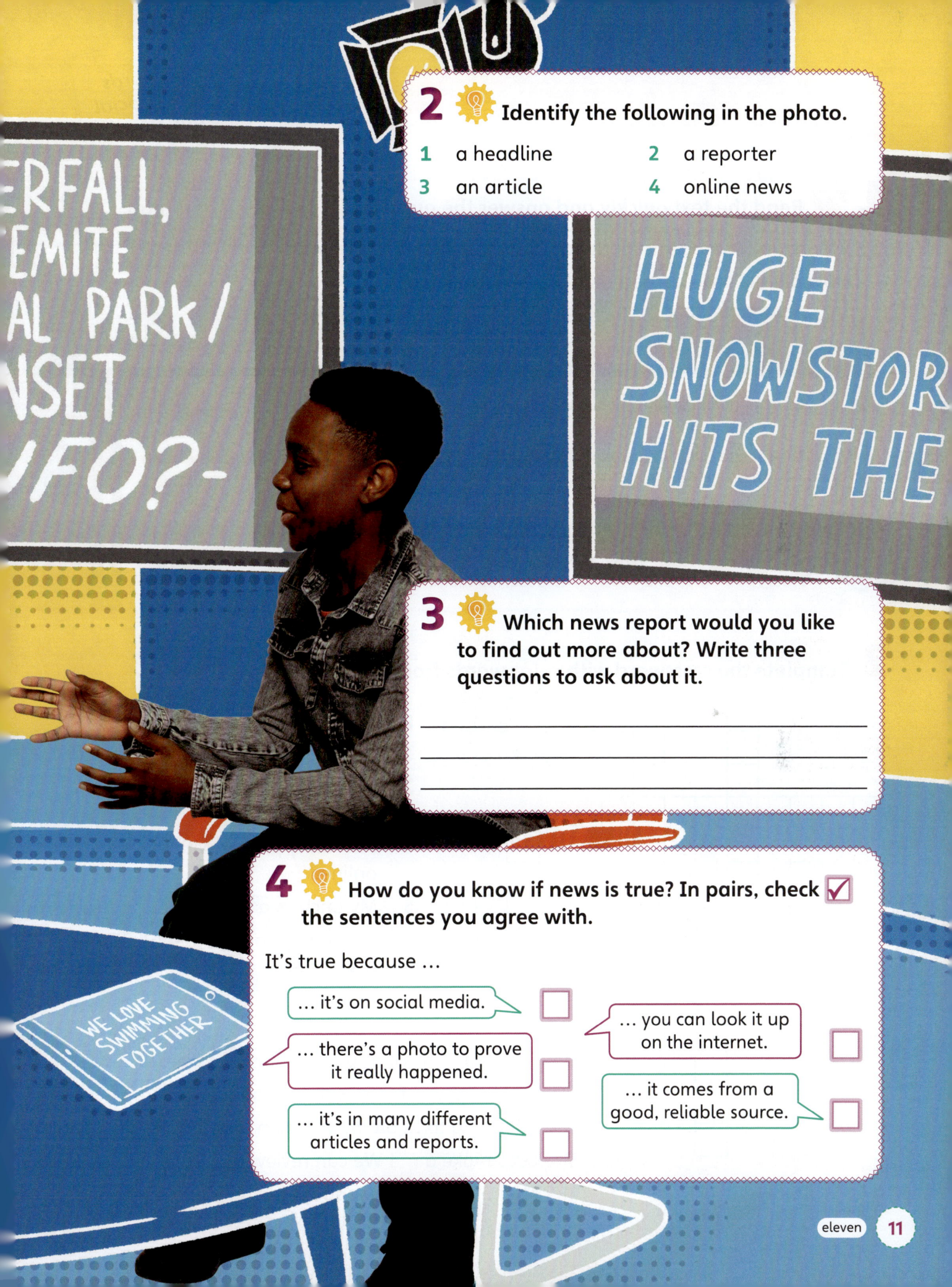

4 How do you know if news is true? In pairs, check ✓ the sentences you agree with.

It's true because …

… it's on social media. ☐

… you can look it up on the internet. ☐

… there's a photo to prove it really happened. ☐

… it comes from a good, reliable source. ☐

… it's in many different articles and reports. ☐

Social media club
VOCABULARY

I will learn words to talk about social media and news.

1 🎧 004 **Read the text quickly and answer the questions. Then listen and read.**

1. Where do the students learn how to make video news reports?
2. How did the teacher learn about news reporting?

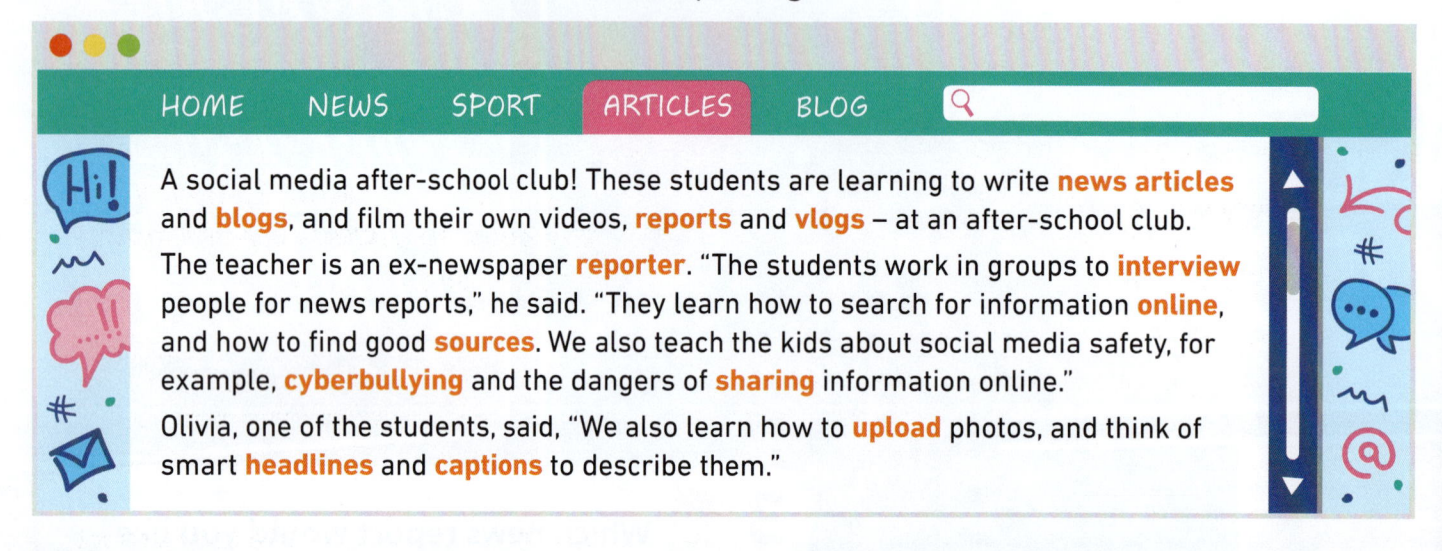

HOME NEWS SPORT **ARTICLES** BLOG 🔍

A social media after-school club! These students are learning to write **news articles** and **blogs**, and film their own videos, **reports** and **vlogs** – at an after-school club.

The teacher is an ex-newspaper **reporter**. "The students work in groups to **interview** people for news reports," he said. "They learn how to search for information **online**, and how to find good **sources**. We also teach the kids about social media safety, for example, **cyberbullying** and the dangers of **sharing** information online."

Olivia, one of the students, said, "We also learn how to **upload** photos, and think of smart **headlines** and **captions** to describe them."

---

2 Complete the crossword with color words from 1.

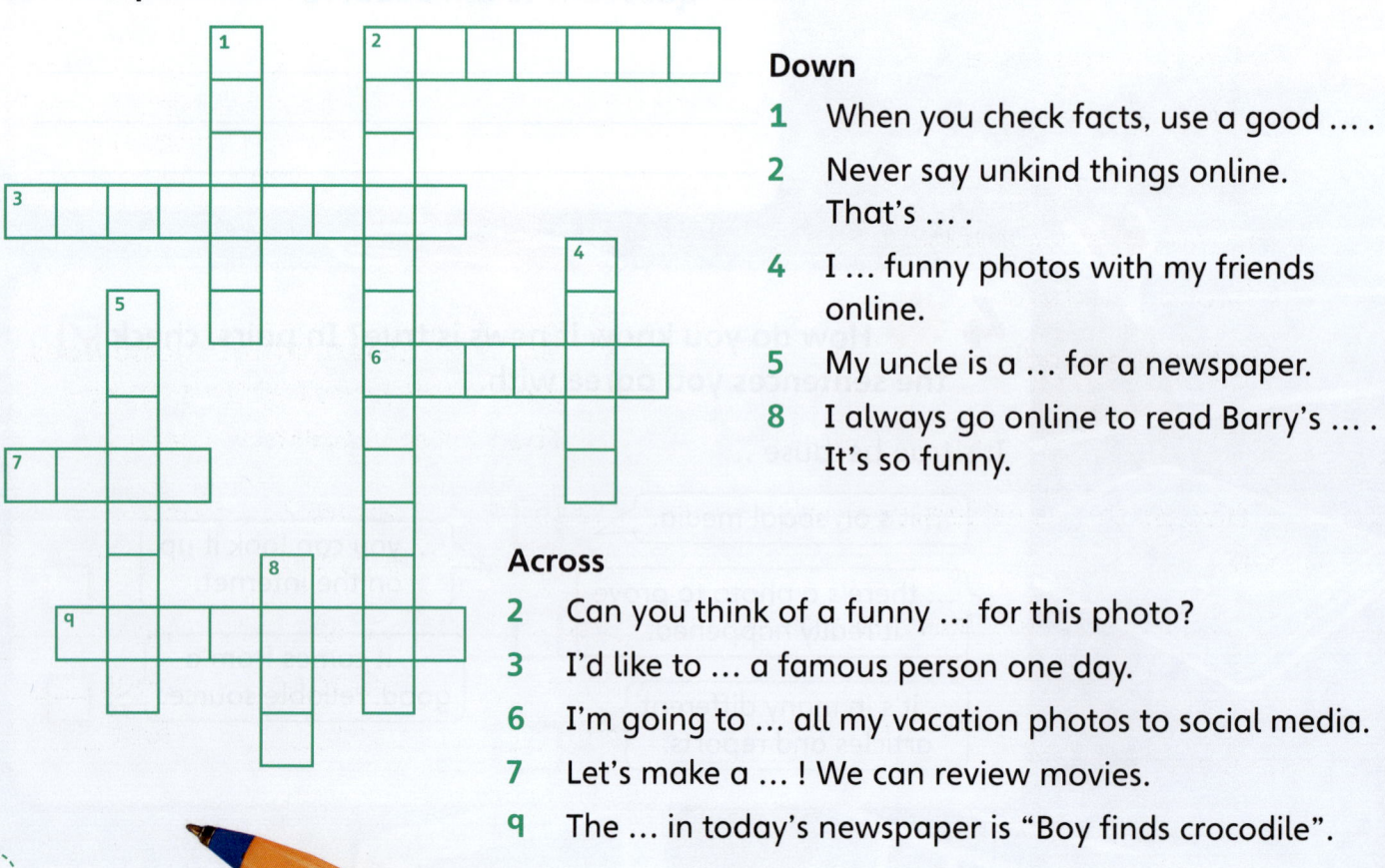

Down
1. When you check facts, use a good … .
2. Never say unkind things online. That's … .
4. I … funny photos with my friends online.
5. My uncle is a … for a newspaper.
8. I always go online to read Barry's … . It's so funny.

Across
2. Can you think of a funny … for this photo?
3. I'd like to … a famous person one day.
6. I'm going to … all my vacation photos to social media.
7. Let's make a … ! We can review movies.
9. The … in today's newspaper is "Boy finds crocodile".

12 twelve

3 Make your own spidergram. Use the color words from 1.

4 Listen and check ✓ the correct box.

1 What does Olivia enjoy most?
 a interviewing people ☐
 b making news reports ☐
 c vlogging ☐

2 How often does she do it?
 a every week ☐
 b every two weeks ☐
 c every day ☐

3 What is it about?
 a reviewing games ☐
 b giving interviews ☐
 c reviewing movies ☐

4 What does Rob want to be?
 a a video games tester ☐
 b a reporter ☐
 c a website designer ☐

5 What is he doing right now?
 a checking the facts ☐
 b writing the headline ☐
 c looking for a good source ☐

5 Discuss the questions in small groups.

1 What would you enjoy most/least about this after-school club? Why?
2 What would you like to make a vlog/write a blog about?

6 Listen to how we say the colored letters. Listen again and repeat.

Let's make a vlog! A lot of people will watch it on the internet.

The after-school club is fun. Why don't you come?

It isn't a good idea to put unkind comments on the internet. That's cyberbullying.

7 Listen. What sound does each word have? Write 1, 2, or 3. Then listen again and check.

Sound 1	Sound 2	Sound 3
watch, vlog	sun, come	good, put

cushion ___   wash ___   money ___
drum ___   shop ___   book ___
blog ___   son ___   foot ___

thirteen 13

Language lab
GRAMMAR 1: REPORTED SPEECH

I will learn to use reported speech.

1 Watch the video.

Direct speech

I watch the news every day.

Vaun

Reported speech

Vaun said that he **watched** the news every day.

I → he/she	my → his/her
you → he/she/they	your → his/her/their
we → they	our → their

2 What did they say? Circle.

Your views ... about the news!

I always read the news because my parents are both reporters!
Amal

We have a funny news story to tell you!
Juan and Maria

I write about news in my blog.
Kai

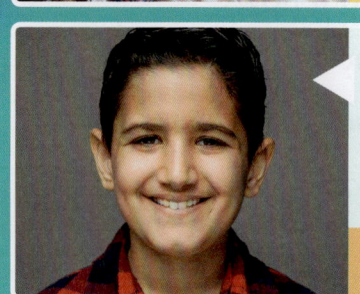

I am interested in sports news.
Hassan

1 Amal said that she always **reads** / **read** the news because her parents **are** / **were** both reporters.
2 Juan and Maria said that they **have** / **had** a funny news story to tell me.
3 Kai said that he **writes** / **wrote** about news in his blog.
4 Hassan said that he **is** / **was** interested in sports news.

3 Look at the picture story. Write the letter.

CODE CRACKER

a   We often rescue cats from trees. I am on my way.
b   I'm stuck in a tree because I'm too scared to climb down!
c   I'm so glad you are safe and back home with me!
d   His name's Gordo. He's really hungry. It's his dinner time.

1 I need help. My cat's stuck in a tree. 1 ___
2 2 ___
3 Gordo! Come for dinner!
4
5 3 ___
6 4 ___

4 Complete the news article. Write the sentences from 3 in reported speech.

LOCAL NEWS — **4TH MARCH**

FIREFIGHTER GETS STUCK IN TREE

A man called the fire service yesterday. He said that
1 _____

The firefighter said that
2 _____

When the firefighter reached the cat, it ran down the tree into the man's arms. He said that
3 _____

The firefighter looked down. He was very high up! He called the fire service, and said that he
4 _____

5 Write one true and one false sentence. Guess if your partner's sentences are true or false.

I have …   I like …
I never …   I often …

Marta
My brother has a pet lizard.

Marta said that her brother had a pet lizard. I think that's true!

Story lab
READING

I will read a mystery story.

1 Look at the picture. Can you guess where in the world Annisa lives? Why do you think this?

2 Read and listen.

The mystery of the missing necklace

The radio was on as Annisa was coming downstairs for breakfast on Saturday. The newsreader was talking about a robbery. Annisa listened while she had her breakfast. The newsreader said that a necklace was missing from Mr. Budi's gift store, in the center of town. The necklace was made of different colored precious stones, and was very expensive.

"Perhaps I can find out who the thief was," thought Annisa. "Then my story will be in the newspaper, and my dream will come true! I'll be a famous reporter!"

She finished her breakfast quickly, got dressed, packed a pencil and a notebook in her backpack, and rode her bike down the hill to the center of town.

3 Circle T (True) or F (False).

1. The theft happened while Annisa was having breakfast. T / F
2. Annisa wanted to be a famous reporter. T / F
3. Annisa lived in the center of town. T / F
4. There were no clues about the thief in the store. T / F
5. The police officer didn't want Annisa to ask any questions. T / F
6. Annisa found the thief before the police. T / F

When she got to Mr. Budi's store, a police officer was there. He was interviewing people about the robbery. They all had different ideas about the thief. One said, "It's someone with short, black hair. I know this because there's short, black hair on the floor." Another said it was someone with very small feet because there were small footprints on the floor.

Annisa went up to them with her notebook and pencil. She wanted to ask them some questions, too, but before she could start, the police officer stopped her.

"I'm sorry, young lady," he said, "but I'm afraid you can't help us. This is a job for the police!"

Annisa was disappointed, but she had another idea. "A good reporter listens and watches," she said to herself, and started looking around carefully for more clues. Then she saw Mr. Budi sitting outdoors, under a tree. She decided to ask him what he thought.

On her way to him, she saw something black in the tree. She looked up and saw a small monkey. As it moved from one branch to another, Annisa noticed, among the green leaves, a flash of color around its neck – blue, red, and yellow …

"I think I've got my story!" she laughed, as she took out her notebook and pencil and started to write.

4 When the police found the necklace, it was broken. Color the missing beads in the correct order.

CODE CRACKER

Values — Fact checking.

5 Think and discuss.

1. How can reporters find out facts?
2. Why is it important for them to check facts before they write an article?
3. What questions should we ask to check facts?

6 What details do you want to change? Act out the story in groups.

7 Make a newspaper bookmark.

Experiment lab
SCIENCE: FREEZING LIQUIDS AND SOLIDS

I will learn about different states of water.

1 Look, think, and discuss. Why do you think this weather story was in the news?

EXTREME ICE STORM HITS USA

Watch a video about states of matter.

2 Read and complete. Then listen and check.

THE CHANGING STATES OF WATER

boiling point   freezing point
gas   liquid   solid

Water is a **1** _____ . When water freezes, it becomes ice. Ice is a **2** _____ . The **3** _____ of water is 0 degrees Celsius. When water is heated to its **4** _____ , 100 degrees Celsius, it becomes water vapour or steam – a **5** _____ .

WHAT HAPPENS WHEN WATER FREEZES?

As a liquid, the molecules in water move around all the time. They crash into each other, and move over and under each other. The molecules in steam can move past each other more easily. They spread out in all directions.

When water freezes, the molecules start to move more slowly, until finally they stop moving. They become hexagonal rings, and when it gets even colder, these hexagonal rings become snowflakes. As water freezes, it expands and takes up more space. It also becomes less dense, or less heavy, than water.

3 Look back at the text in 2 and label the diagrams.

ice   water   steam

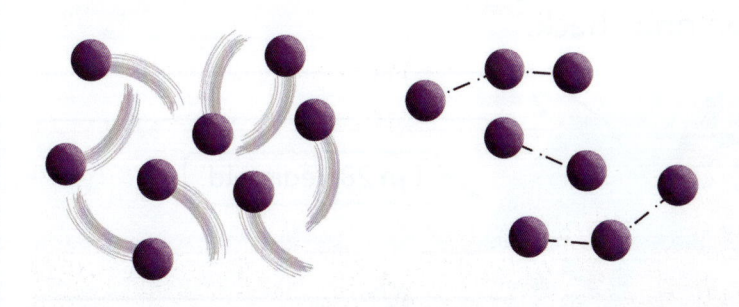

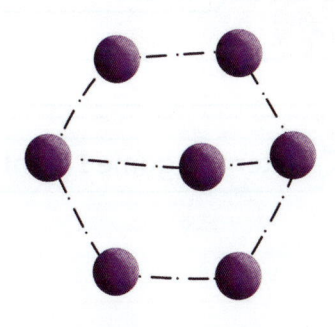

1 _____   2 _____

3 _____

4 Work in pairs and discuss.

1 In cold countries people put salt on the road when ice might form. Why do you think they do that?
2 Why does ice float on top of water?

5 Circle T (True) or F (False).

1 Water molecules move more slowly than ice molecules.   T / F
2 Water molecules remain in one position.   T / F
3 Ice molecules are organized in shapes.   T / F
4 The molecules in ice are further apart than in water.   T / F

6 Figure it out! Compare with a partner.

MATH ZONE

1 There are 10 cm of snow on the ground. How many more centimeters of snow need to fall for the snow to reach the top of your head?
2 The snow melts away by 2 cm every day. How many days will it take to disappear?

EXPERIMENT TIME

What happens when you freeze different materials?

Materials
- 3 paper cups
- a teaspoon of salt
- a teaspoon of food coloring
- a can of soda

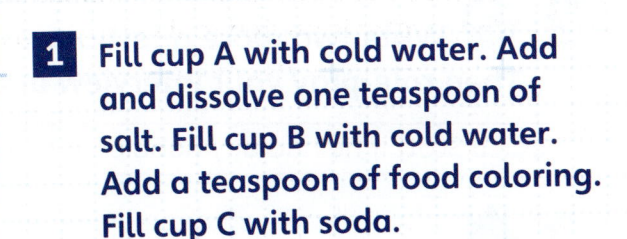

1 Fill cup A with cold water. Add and dissolve one teaspoon of salt. Fill cup B with cold water. Add a teaspoon of food coloring. Fill cup C with soda.
2 Put all the cups in the freezer for a day.
3 Predict what will happen to the liquid in each cup. What are the results?

nineteen 19

He asked me if …

COMMUNICATION: REPORTED SPEECH QUESTIONS

I will learn about reporting an interview.

1 Look at the sentences. Can you guess the questions the reporters asked Scott? Write. Then listen and check.

1 _____
I'm from Boston, USA!

2 _____
I'm 28 years old.

3 _____
My birthday's in January.

4 _____
Spaghetti and meatballs!

5 _____
No, I don't watch much TV.

6 _____
After the game I want to sleep!

	Direct questions	Reported speech questions
Wh- questions	Where are you from?	They asked him where he was from.
Yes/No questions	Do you like our city?	They asked him if he liked their city.

2 Write two more questions to ask Scott. Then role-play your interview and report back to the class.

I asked Scott if he had any hobbies. He said he liked listening to music.

3 Interview classmates for a school magazine. In your notebooks, write direct questions.

4 Work in groups and ask your questions. Then tell the class who asked you what.

Do you have any brothers and sisters?

Leon asked me if I had any brothers and sisters.

What time do you get up in the morning?

Gita asked me what time I got up in the morning.

20 twenty

Writing lab
WRITING A PODCAST

I will write a podcast.

1 💡 Look at the photo and the headline. What do you think the podcast is about?

2 Read the podcast script and answer the Wh- questions in your notebook.

> A good news report answers these five Wh- questions:
> - **Who** (or **what**) is the story about?
> - **What** happened?
> - **When** did it happen?
> - **Where** did it happen?
> - **Why** did the story end well?

HOME | VIDEOS | BOOKS | STORE

SPEAKER	TEXT
Presenter:	**ANIMALS RESCUE SURFER FROM DANGER**
Presenter:	A young surfer had a lucky escape yesterday thanks to some friendly dolphins. Sandy Rider, 12, was in the ocean at Long Beach, California, when he saw a shark's fin just a few meters away from him. But before the shark could reach Sandy, a group of dolphins appeared. They swam around Sandy, forming a ring around him, and the shark couldn't touch him. The amazing animal rescuers followed Sandy all the way to the beach, where he was safe. Sandy said that from that moment on, dolphins had a special place in his heart. Our reporter spoke to Sandy later.
Reporter:	How did you feel when you saw the shark, Sandy?
Sandy:	I was terrified! I wanted to swim away, but I couldn't move.
Presenter:	That was our reporter talking to Sandy Rider. Later, he said that he wanted to start a Save the Dolphins group on social media. After all, they saved his life!

Sandy Rider, 12

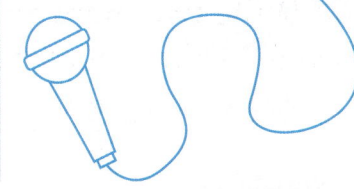

3 Find and underline the following in the podcast script.

1. headline 2. a caption 3. a fact 4. direct speech 5. reported speech

4 💬 Use the five Wh- questions to plan and write a script for a podcast news report. Then read your script in groups.

twenty-one 21

PROJECT AND REVIEW

Make a video news report

Step 1

Research

▸ Where can we find the news?

- [ ] Work in pairs.
- [ ] Make a list of different ways to find out about the news. How are they different?
- [ ] Choose two or three stories you find interesting.
- [ ] Collect photos, pictures, and headlines about the stories.

How we find out about the news:

- newspapers
- online video site
- websites

Step 2

Plan

▸ How do we check facts?

- [ ] Form a group and compare your stories.
- [ ] Find the answers to the Wh- questions.
- [ ] Check the facts! Compare different sources.
- [ ] Decide who to interview for your news report. What are they going to talk about?

Who?   What?   When?
Where?   Why?

Interview 1: the girl

I was walking my dog on Shelley Beach, when …

Interview 2: a history expert

We studied the coin at the museum and found that it comes from the Roman period …

22   twenty-two

Step 3
Create

> How do we report the news?

- ☐ Write the text for your report.
- ☐ How are you going to introduce your story? Think of a way to make your story interesting.
- ☐ Include all the facts, using your Wh- questions.
- ☐ Report what people said.
- ☐ Decide different roles for each person in your group.
- ☐ Practice giving your report.
- ☐ Record your report.

Introduction: Do you ever dream about finding something really valuable one day? That's exactly what happened to Mia Jackson, 12, when she was walking her dog …

Interview 1: Our reporter, Sebastian, asked Mia how she felt. She said she was very excited because a museum wanted to display the coin.

Watch the news at home with your family or friends. When you hear a headline, see if you can guess what the story is about.

Step 4
Show and tell

> Show your video report to the class.

- ☐ Discuss the videos.
- ☐ Which were most interesting? Why?
- ☐ What kind of sources did they use?

Now I can …

- … use words to talk about social media and the news.
- … use reported speech.
- … use reported speech questions.
- … write a script for a podcast news report.

twenty-three 23

2 Inspirational people

How can I make a book of inspirational people?

1 Look and discuss. Do you know any of the people in the photo?

2 💡 Look at the characteristics and think of someone you know for each one.

brave
compassionate
inspirational
intelligent
kind

3 💬 Write jobs on sticky notes. Choose one you think is inspirational.

4 💡 Discuss your choice in **3**.

I think vets are inspirational because they care for animals.

I think scientists are inspirational because they find cures for diseases.

Inspirational people
VOCABULARY

I will learn words to describe people and their jobs.

1 🔧 **Read the text quickly and answer the questions. Then listen and read.**

1. What is Claudia and Luis's project about?
2. Who does Claudia think Luis should write about?

Claudia: Hi Luis, who are you going to write about for your project on **inspirational** people?

Luis: I'm not sure – there are so many to choose from! I might write about Michelle Obama.

Claudia: But we can't write about politicians.

Luis: She's not a politician. She used to be a **lawyer**, but now she's an **author** and a **campaigner**. She's a very **determined** person and she promotes education for girls around the world. What about you?

Claudia: I want to write about a famous scientist. Someone really **intelligent** like Stephen Hawking or Einstein. I might write about a **researcher** like Jane Goodall.

Luis: What did she research?

Claudia: She researched chimpanzees. She was very **brave** to go near them in the wild.

Luis: I might write about my Uncle Ricardo. He's not famous, but he's **compassionate** and very **generous**.

Claudia: Wow – what does he do?

Luis: He's a **charity worker**. He works as a **volunteer** for a charity that helps children.

Claudia: Definitely write about Uncle Ricardo!

2 💡 **Which jobs and characteristics are important? List and discuss with a partner.**

> author   brave   campaigner   charity worker   compassionate   determined
> generous   inspirational   intelligent   lawyer   researcher   volunteer

	More important					Less important
Jobs	___	___	___	___	___	___
Characteristics	___	___	___	___	___	___

3 Listen and circle T (True) or F (False).

1. Daniel agrees that lawyers are determined people. **T / F**
2. Kim thinks law school is easy. **T / F**
3. Kim doesn't think Daniel is intelligent. **T / F**
4. Kim wants to research cures for diseases. **T / F**
5. Daniel thinks researchers who find cures for diseases are inspirational. **T / F**
6. All charity workers are volunteers. **T / F**

Values — Value yourself.

I think I'm generous, determined, and funny.

Yes, you are!

4 Read and do.

Think: What are your best characteristics?
Pair: Talk about your best characteristics with a partner.
Share: Share your ideas with the class. Did anyone else put the same characteristics as you?

5 Create a spidergram to help you remember the new words.

6 Listen and sort. Then say the words.

beach   clean   eat
feathers   head   healthy
read   sea   wealthy

short ea — **both** — **long ea**

7 Look at the codes. Circle the bugs. Listen and check.

CODE CRACKER

short ea
heavy   head   wealthy
eat   bread   breakfast
weather   bead

long ea
beach   head   pea
dream   feathers   clean
tea   team

twenty-seven 27

Language lab
GRAMMAR 1: RELATIVE CLAUSES

I will learn to use relative clauses.

1 Watch the video.

People	She's the woman	**who/that**	works as a charity worker.
Things and animals	That's the book	**which/that**	sold a million copies.
Places	This is	**where**	the politician lived.
Times	That was the day	**when**	they finally won their campaign.
Possessions	He's a researcher	**whose**	discoveries changed the world.

Look out! Whose and **who's** (who is) sound the same.

2 Look at the pictures. Then match them to the sentences in **3**.

a   b   c   d

3 Read and circle.

1 She's an ecologist (whose / who) is campaigning against palm oil plantations.
2 The charity (that / who) he volunteers for cleans plastic trash off beaches.
3 A laboratory is a place (where / which) researchers work.
4 Is that the man (that / whose) book has sold a million copies?

4 Read and match.

1 This is a book
2 She is the girl
3 A school is the place
4 That's the horse
5 That was the year

- where
- when
- that
- who
- that

- helps her friends.
- he owns.
- describes the author's life.
- I turned 11.
- we learn English.

5 Read and complete with relative pronouns.

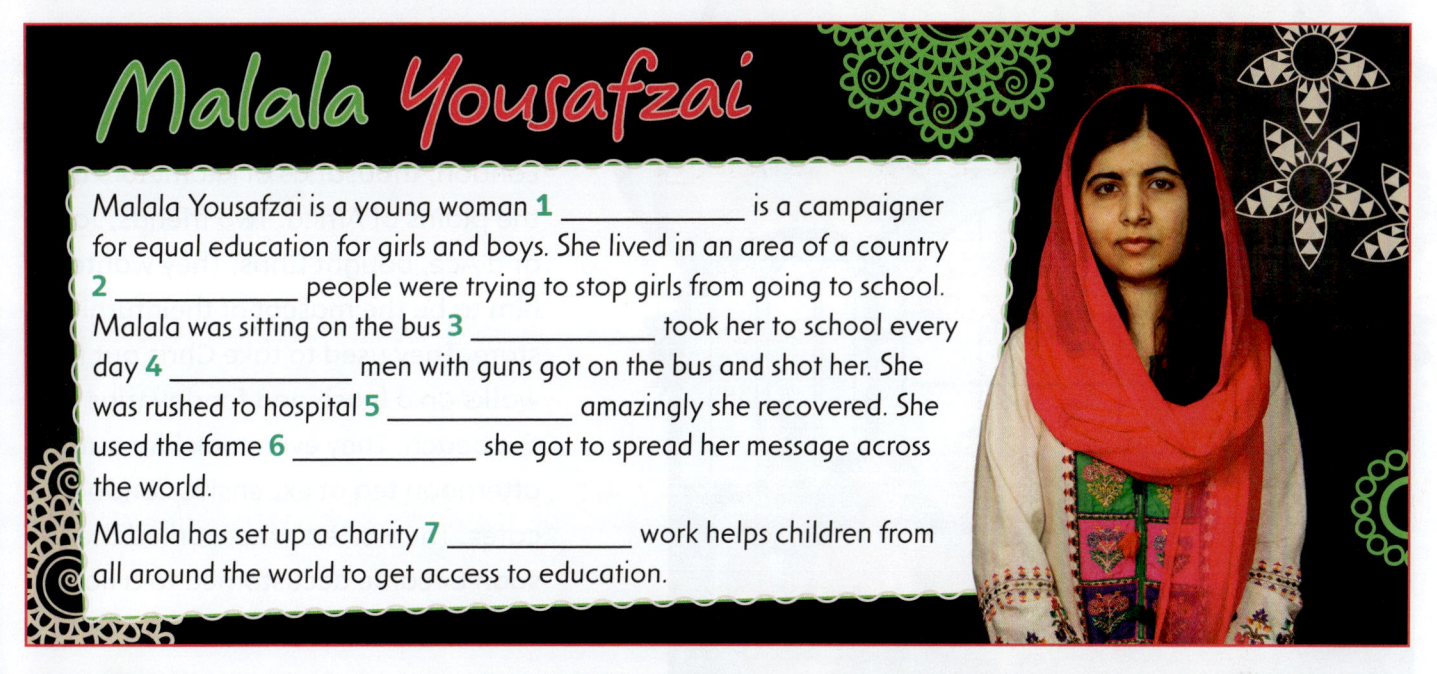

Malala Yousafzai

Malala Yousafzai is a young woman **1** _____ is a campaigner for equal education for girls and boys. She lived in an area of a country **2** _____ people were trying to stop girls from going to school. Malala was sitting on the bus **3** _____ took her to school every day **4** _____ men with guns got on the bus and shot her. She was rushed to hospital **5** _____ amazingly she recovered. She used the fame **6** _____ she got to spread her message across the world.
Malala has set up a charity **7** _____ work helps children from all around the world to get access to education.

6 Create the cover for your own autobiography. Then think of a title.

7 Complete sentences in your own words using relative pronouns.

1 Compassionate describes a person _____ .
2 A biography is a book _____ .
3 A law court is a place _____ .
4 _____ job is to help protect animals and their habitats.
5 An inspirational person is a person _____ .

8 Play Descriptions game.

This is a person who looks after people in the hospital.

A nurse?

twenty-nine 29

Story lab
READING

I will read a biographical story.

1 Look at the pictures. Do you think this story really happened or is it fictional?

2 Read and listen. Check your answer to **1**.

THE HUGGING LION

Joy and George Adamson were big cat conservationists and campaigners who lived in Kenya, Africa. They were famous for raising a lion cub, called Elsa, who was orphaned when her mother was shot. Joy was very compassionate about lions and, although she loved Elsa, she wanted to set her free so she could live a natural life in the wild. Joy, who was also an author and artist, wrote a book about Elsa called *Born Free* which later inspired a movie of the same name. But Elsa wasn't the only notable lion that came into the Adamson's life …

Once upon a time, there was a lion cub called Chris. Chris was in the pet store of a department store in London, thousands of kilometers from the plains of Africa. Two friends, John and Ace, bought Chris. They wanted him to be the mascot of their furniture store. They used to take Chris out for walks on a leash and for day trips to the beach. They even took him out for afternoon tea at expensive London cafés. The waiters who worked there soon became accustomed to a lion coming for tea!

Chris grew bigger and bigger, but he loved his owners very much. One day, by complete coincidence, the actors who played Joy and George Adamson in the movie *Born Free* visited John and Ace's furniture store. They saw Chris and told John and Ace all about the Adamsons' work. They suggested that they took Chris to the Adamsons' reserve in Kenya where he could be introduced to life in the wild just like Elsa. John and Ace were sad, but they knew it was best for Chris.

A year later, John and Ace went to visit their old pet who was now free with his own group of lions. They didn't know what Chris would do when he saw them again; they were very brave (and perhaps foolish) to walk up to a fully-grown male lion! Suddenly, Chris ran towards his old friends. Was he going to attack them? No! He put his huge paws on their shoulders and hugged them just like he used to when he was their pet lion in London. Like Elsa, this meeting made Chris a movie star – the video clip of him hugging John and Ace has been watched by millions of people online!

3 Read the text again and answer the questions.

1. Which job didn't Joy Adamson do?
   a artist   b actress   c author   d campaigner
2. Where did John and Ace get Chris?
   a a reserve in Africa   b a furniture store
   c a department store   d a café
3. What didn't Chris do in London?
   a go on a bus   b take walks on a leash
   c be the mascot for a furniture store   d go to cafés
4. What did Chris do when he saw John and Ace in Africa?
   a run away   b bite them   c ignore them   d hug them

4 Think and discuss.

1. Why do you think John and Ace wanted Chris to live in Africa?
2. Do you think Chris was happier in London or Africa? Why?
3. What animals are not suitable pets? Why?

5 Think of a new ending for the story. Act out the story in groups.

Experiment lab
SCIENCE: MOLD AND BACTERIA

I will learn about mold and bacteria.

1 Look at the microscope slides. Which is the odd one out?

Watch a video about bacteria and germs.

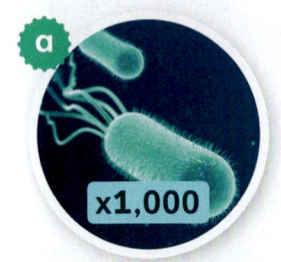

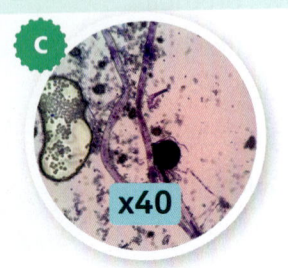

a x1,000
b x1,000
c x40
d x1,000

2 Read about mold and bacteria. Look at **1**. Which one is mold?

CODE CRACKER

- Bacteria are tiny! You can't see them without a microscope.
- You can't see individual mold particles without a microscope, but you can see mold without a microscope when the particles grow together.

3 Read and calculate.

MATH ZONE

How big will the particle look under these microscopes?

a x7
b x10
c x40

32 thirty-two

4 Read and listen. What did Alexander Fleming discover?

ALEXANDER FLEMING

I think an inspirational person from history is Dr. Alexander Fleming. He was a scientific researcher who was determined to find a cure for bacterial diseases which killed millions of people every year. In the end, he found the cure by accident!

Dr. Fleming had a lot of dishes of bacteria in his lab, and he didn't clean up much! One day, when he came back from vacation, he saw mold growing on one of his dirty dishes. Under the microscope he saw that there was no bacteria growing around the mold. With more investigation, he discovered that something in the mold killed bacteria.

It took many more years to make the mold into an antibiotic medicine, but it was the start of something that has saved millions of lives!

5 Read again. Circle T (True) or F (False).

1. Alexander Fleming wasn't trying to find a cure for bacterial disease. T / F
2. The mold was killing the bacteria. T / F
3. Alexander Fleming made an antibiotic medicine straight away. T / F

EXPERIMENT TIME

Materials
slices of bread   plastic zip bags

Which conditions does mold grow best in?

1. Sprinkle water on three slices of bread and leave three slices dry.
2. Put each slice of bread in a plastic zip bag. Seal and tape each bag.
3. Pair up the bags – one with damp and one with dry bread.
4. Put one pair of bags in a fridge, one pair at room temperature, and one pair in a warm place.
5. Predict which slice of bread will grow the most mold.
6. Test your predictions.

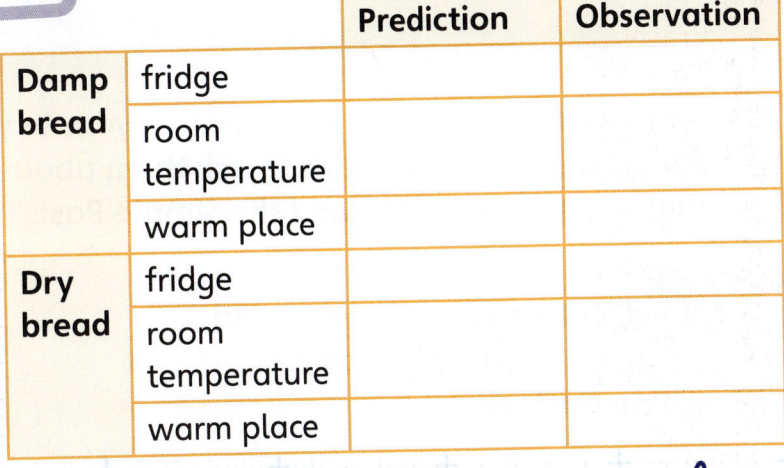

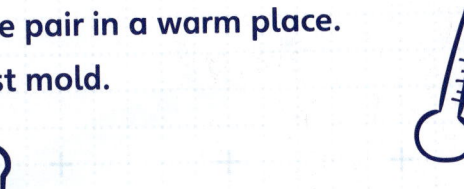

		Prediction	Observation
Damp bread	fridge		
	room temperature		
	warm place		
Dry bread	fridge		
	room temperature		
	warm place		

Being different!

COMMUNICATION: *USED TO*

I will learn how to talk about past habits and states.

1 🎧 017 **Listen. Who's Chloe talking to? Check ✓.**

a her grandpa ☐   b her dad ☐   c her uncle ☐

2 Listen again and answer.

1 Grandpa used to live in …
   a a different town.   b a different neighborhood.   c the same house as now.
2 Black and white children used to …
   a go to different schools.   b go to the same school.   c all be friends.
3 Grandpa used to go to the movies …
   a with his kids.   b every Friday night.   c with Grandma.

3 💬 **Answer the question. Then ask a partner.**

1 What games did you use to play?
   _____
2 Did you use to study another language?
   _____
3 What food didn't you use to eat?
   _____

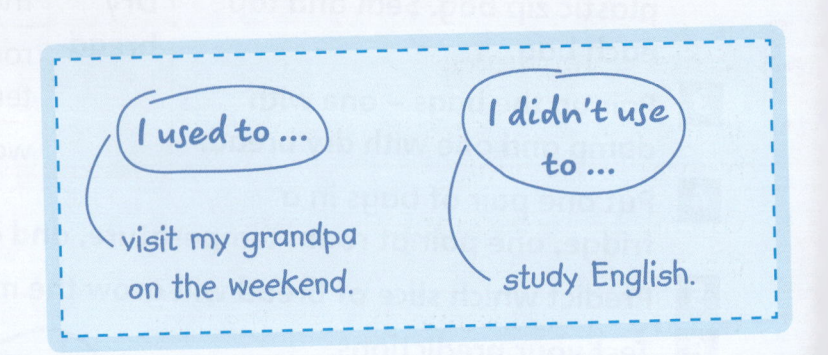

I	used to	live in Texas.
She	didn't use to	go to school.
Did you	use to	study English?

4 🌟 **Think of a relative who inspires you. In your notebook, write questions to ask them about their past. Use used to and the Simple Past.**

Where did you use to work?
Where did you study?

5 💬 **List things you used to and didn't use to do. Then discuss with a partner.**

I used to … visit my grandpa on the weekend.

I didn't use to … study English.

34 thirty-four

Writing lab
WRITING A BIOGRAPHY

I will write a biography of someone I know.

1 Look at the photo and read the biography quickly. Who wrote it?

MY GRANDPA

The person who inspires me most is my grandpa.

My grandpa used to live in a very different time to now. When he was my age, black kids couldn't go to school with white kids. That meant that my grandpa didn't get a good education.

When he was a young man he worked as a laborer, but he dreamed of being a lawyer or a politician. He decided to study law at college. It was hard work, but he was determined, and after graduating college, he became a lawyer. Many years later, he became a senator in Arkansas.

My grandpa is an intelligent man who has worked hard to achieve his dreams. However, more importantly, he's a fun grandpa who loves his family!

2 Underline the words and phrases Chloe uses to link ideas.

1. Which word or phrase contrasts ideas between sentences?
2. Which word or phrase contrasts ideas within a sentence?
3. Which words or phrases show the passage of time?

> Use *after* or *before* + *-ing* to show the order of events.
>
> Before working as a lawyer, he worked as a laborer.
> After graduating college, he became a lawyer.

3 Write a biography.

- In the first sentence, sum up who your biography is about.
- Use relative pronouns to give extra information.
- Use *used to* to describe things in the past.
- Use words and phrases to link ideas.

4 Draw or take a photo of the person you wrote about. Create a classroom display and share your stories.

thirty-five 35

PROJECT AND REVIEW

Make a class book of inspirational people

Step 1

Research

> Find out about an inspirational person.

- ☐ Think of a famous and/or historical person who inspires you.
- ☐ Research his/her life. Think of how you can describe the person and how they inspire you.
- ☐ Play a guessing game with a partner. Can they guess your person?

"I chose someone who is very determined and very, very fast. He's from Jamaica."

"Usain Bolt?"

"Yes!"

Step 2

Plan

> Make a spidergram for your biography.

- ☐ Choose the most interesting and inspiring things to write about your person.
- ☐ Make your plan.

Frida Kahlo
- artist
- lived in a blue house
- married Diego Rivera
- painted in bed
- determined
- talented
- had a bus accident
- brave
- painted lots of self-portraits

36 thirty-six

Step 3

Create

> Write your biography.

- ☐ Think about how to describe people, things, and places using relative clauses.
- ☐ Think about how to talk about the past.
- ☐ Remember to say why your person is inspirational.
- ☐ Include the most interesting things in their life.
- ☐ Create a portrait of your person.
- ☐ Compile all your biographies and portraits into a class book.

Read a book about an inspirational person.

Step 4

Show and tell

> Present your page of the class book.

Stephen Hawking was a physicist and researcher who was very intelligent. He wrote books which explained some of the mysteries of the universe. He used to live in Cambridge in the U.K. where he worked at the university.

Now I can ...

- ... use words to talk about inspirational people and their jobs.
- ... use relative clauses.
- ... use *used to* to talk about the past.
- ... write a biography.

thirty-seven 37

1 Checkpoint
UNITS 1 AND 2

1 🎧 018 Listen and complete the quiz for Anya. What is her perfect job?

What is your PERFECT JOB?

1 What's the most important thing for you about a job?
- A I want to volunteer with animals.
- B I want to travel and see the world.
- C I want to help people.

2 Which topic do you worry about most?
- A We are in danger of losing 40 percent of the world's wildlife.
- B 17 percent of people under 25 experience cyberbullying.
- C One in nine people don't have fresh water close to their homes.

3 Which sentence describes you best?
- A I'm brave and not afraid of danger.
- B I'm interested in other people.
- C I'm kind and compassionate.

4 Which sentence best describes your media habits?
- A Social media apps are becoming more popular than other news sources.
- B The most reliable sources of news are newspapers, then online search engines, and lastly, social media sites.
- C Young people listen to more podcasts than live radio shows.

5 What was the last piece of writing that you did?
- A I wrote an email.
- B I wrote a text message.
- C I wrote a story.

6 When I was very young, I used to want to be …
- A a conservationist.
- B a pilot.
- C a nurse or a doctor.

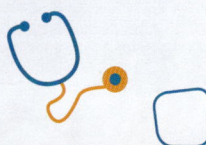

Now find out your results!

Mostly As You care about animals and the environment. You want to try to change the world. You should consider being a lawyer or a campaigner.

Mostly Bs Social media motivates you! You use it to follow the news and to tell people about yourself. You should consider being a reporter or traveling the world as a vlogger.

Mostly Cs You are generous and helpful. You care about other people's problems. You should consider being a teacher or charity worker.

thirty-eight

2 Read the quiz again and write *True, False* or *Can't say*.

CODE CRACKER

1. Less than half of the world's wildlife population is in danger of becoming extinct. _____
2. Cyberbullying happens to almost all young people at some time. _____
3. The number of people without fresh water will increase in the future. _____
4. More people trust online search engines for news than social media sites. _____
5. Podcasts are more popular with young people than with older people. _____

3 Complete the questions about something that happened to Vaun. Then answer the questions and write a short newspaper article.

1. _____Who/What_____ is the story about? _____
2. _____ happened? _____
3. When _____ happen? _____
4. _____ it happen? _____
5. _____ did the story end? _____

Tuesday 3:15 p.m.

Tuesday 5:35 p.m.

4 Look back at the quiz. Ask and answer with a partner. Find out how many of your classmates have the same results as you.

You got mostly As. You should be a lawyer!

thirty-nine 39

Sweden
CULTURE

Sweden

Sweden is a country in northern Europe. The capital city of Sweden is Stockholm. Stockholm is built on 14 islands and has more than 50 bridges. Because it's near the Arctic Circle, Sweden has long, light days in summer, but it has very short days in winter. Sweden is famous for an award called the Nobel Prize.

Fun Fact!

About 400,000 moose live wild in Sweden. The moose is the largest member of the deer family.

1 019 Read and listen. Which are not Nobel Prize categories? Check ✓.

Chemistry ☐   Peace ☐   Ecology ☐
Medicine ☐   Literature ☐   Physics ☐

THE NOBEL PRIZE
Home | About | Events

Alfred Nobel was a Swedish inventor who left all his money to give prizes for amazing achievements in physics, chemistry, medicine, literature, and for work in peace.

Alfred Nobel was born in Stockholm, Sweden, in 1833. He spoke several languages, wrote poetry and was very interested in social, health, and peace-related issues. He worked as an engineer, a chemist, and an inventor. His most famous invention was dynamite. He invented dynamite to use in engineering, but it was also used in war. This is another reason Nobel wanted to give prizes for positive achievements, including work for peace. He wanted to be remembered for good things!

Unfortunately, Nobel wasn't alive to see the prizes start. The prizes started in 1901 which was five years after he died. Since then 935 men, women, and organizations from all around the world have won the prize including Albert Einstein, Marie Sklodowska-Curie, Martin Luther King, and Nelson Mandela. One thing all Nobel Prize winners, who are called "laureates", have in common is that they are inspirational people.

2 Read again. Circle T (True) or F (False).

1 Nobel's money is used to fund prizes. T / F
2 Nobel was born in the capital city of Sweden. T / F
3 The categories of the Nobel Prize reflect Nobel's interests. T / F
4 The prizes started when Nobel was alive. T / F
5 Nobel laureates are all from Sweden. T / F

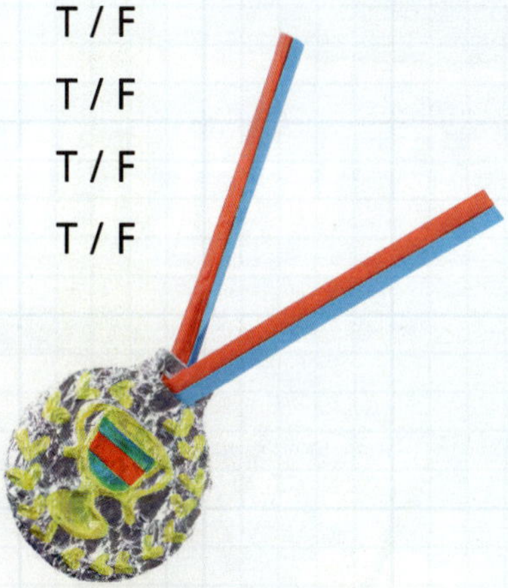

3 Create a medal for your own award.

4 Present your medal to someone in the class.

> The person who wins my special García award for most helpful classmate is …

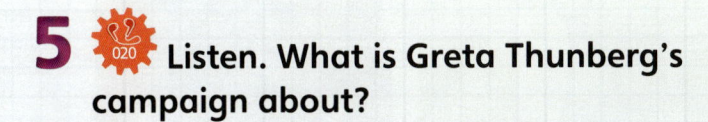

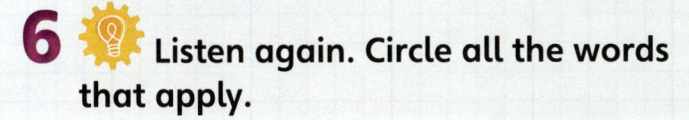

5 Listen. What is Greta Thunberg's campaign about?

6 Listen again. Circle all the words that apply.

1 Greta Thunberg is a …   politician   lawyer   student
2 Greta started her
  campaign …   alone   with a friend with her class
3 Now she speaks to …   politicians   reporters   journalists
4 I think Greta is very …   determined   compassionate inspirational

My Culture

7 Read and discuss.

1 Have you seen Greta Thunberg or Malala Yousafzai on the news or read about them in the newspaper?
2 Why do you think they are inspirational to young people?
3 Can you think of any inspirational people from you country? Why are they inspirational?

Malala Yousafzai – Pakistan

forty-one 41

3 Let's earn money!

How can I make an advertisement for my business?

DOG WALKING

Face Painting
$5.00

Balloon Animals
$2.50 per animal

Balloon Animals and Face Painting

Prices
Lemonade $1.00
Muffin (chocolate, chocolate chip) $1.50
Cookie $1.00

1 Look and discuss. Which activities at the fair do you think could earn the most money?

2 **Think and discuss.**

> bake cookies   design a T-shirt   do face painting
> make balloon models   sell lemonade   walk dogs
> make brownies

1 Which other ideas do you think could be good business ideas? Why?
2 How can you earn money from these ideas?
3 What would you spend money on at a fair like this?

3 **Complete the chants about the activities in 2. Listen and check. Then say the activity.**

> long   sweet   tight

It's made of plastic, bright and light.
It's full of air, but you must hold it 1 _____ !

It's fresh and tasty, nice and 2 _____ .
The perfect drink for the summer heat.

Smooth, dark chocolate, but it's not a cake.
Guess how 3 _____ it took us to make!

4 **Choose another activity from 2. Work with a partner to write a chant about it. Can the class guess the activity?**

forty-three 43

Young people in business
VOCABULARY

I will learn words to talk about money.

1 Read the text quickly. Which three activities does it describe?

Meet the winners of our People in Business awards!

Julia: I love baking. One day, for our school sports day, I decorated some cookies with our team colors. They didn't cost very much and everyone wanted to buy one. Now I decorate and **sell** cookies for a lot of different special events.

Miguel: A few weeks ago, just for fun, I made a vlog. I reviewed a new video game. A lot of people liked watching it, so I started reviewing different **products**. I am **saving** to buy my own webcam, and I might even **invent** my own game.

Carmen: I often walk my dogs so my mom said, "You could start a dog-walking business and **earn** some extra **cash**!" I liked the idea so I made an **advertisement**. Now I do a few dog walks every weekend. It's fun and I listen to podcasts while I walk! You don't have to **spend** a lot of money. There are lower **prices** for short walks.

2 Read the text again and circle T (True) or F (False).

1. Julia's sports day cookies were expensive. T / F
2. Julia sells cookies in different team colors. T / F
3. Miguel doesn't spend his money. T / F
4. He has his own webcam. T / F
5. Carmen tells people about her dog-walking business through podcasts. T / F

3 Circle the correct word.

1. My brother (spends / saves) all his money on comics! I think he should (sell / save) his money for something special.
2. I'm trying to think of a (success / product) to (spend / invent) for a competition.
3. I'm going to (earn / sell) these old games to (invent / earn) some extra (cash / prices).
4. I'm going to write (a product / an advertisement) for my school bulletin board.
5. How much are these bracelets? Are they all the same (cash / price)?

4 Write sentences with the color words from 1.

5 Listen and check ✓.

1 Which product did Richie invent?

a ☐   b ☐   c ☐

2 What was Richie doing when he had the idea for his product?

a ☐   b ☐   c ☐

3 What was Richie doing when he missed an important TV show?

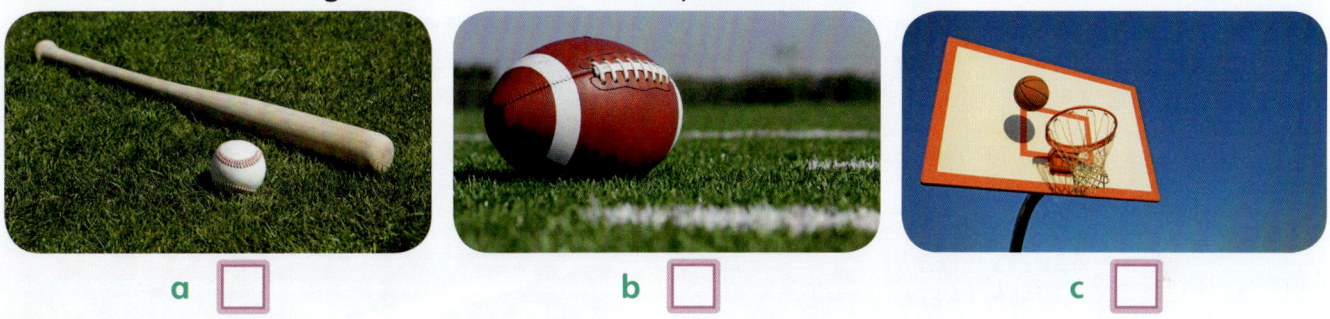

a ☐   b ☐   c ☐

6 Work in pairs. Think, talk, and imagine.

1 What do you like spending money on?
2 What would you like to save money for? How do you think you could earn some extra cash?

7 Make a money box. Recycle a cardboard container. Save spare coins!

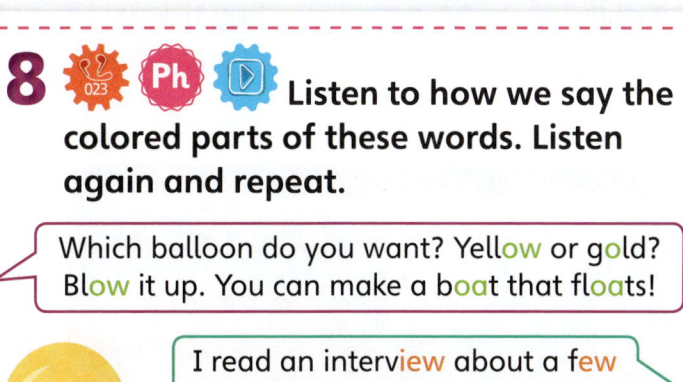

8 Listen to how we say the colored parts of these words. Listen again and repeat.

Which balloon do you want? Yellow or gold? Blow it up. You can make a boat that floats!

I read an interview about a few kids who started a business.

Did you design that blue T-shirt – and those new shoes?

forty-five 45

Language lab
GRAMMAR 1: OBLIGATION AND ADVICE

I will learn how to talk about obligation and advice.

1 Watch the video.

> should/shouldn't = advice:
>   You **should** listen to the rules of the game.
> have to = strong obligation:
>   You **have to** pay with cash.
> don't have to = not necessary:
>   You **don't have to** buy all the cookies.
> must/mustn't = strong obligation:
>   You **must** stand in line.

2 Complete the rules for the school fair. Write have to, don't have to, must, mustn't, should, or shouldn't.

1 Adults ___have to___ buy tickets.
   Children _____ buy tickets.

2 You _____ throw the ball too high! And you _____ stand behind the line.

3 Before you play the game, you _____ think carefully. Choose the prize you want to win!

4 You _____ eat too much candy! It will make you sick.

46 forty-six

3 Look at the poster. Complete the sentences. Then listen and check.

> don't have to (2)   must   mustn't   should   shouldn't

We're having a SCHOOL FAIR!

✓ **Do** come and earn some money or spend some cash!

✗ **Don't** forget to tell your parents and friends!

👎 **It's NOT a good idea to** sell broken toys.

👍 **It's a good idea to** have lots of prizes for competitions.

🙂 **It's OK. You can** bring your own food and drink.

1 You ___don't have to___ sell things, but you _____ come to the fair and earn some money or spend some cash!

2 The fair is for everyone so you _____ forget to tell your parents and friends.

3 You _____ sell broken toys.

4 You _____ have lots of prizes for people to win.

5 You _____ buy anything to eat or drink. You can bring your own!

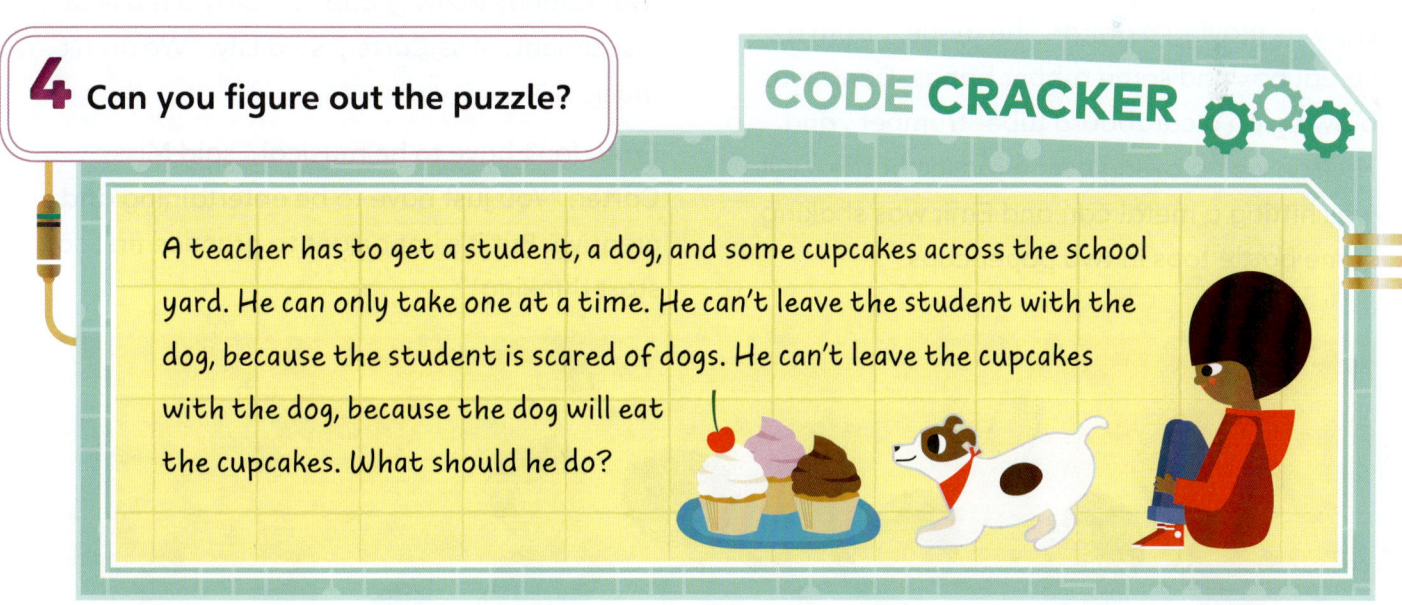

4 Can you figure out the puzzle?

CODE CRACKER

A teacher has to get a student, a dog, and some cupcakes across the school yard. He can only take one at a time. He can't leave the student with the dog, because the student is scared of dogs. He can't leave the cupcakes with the dog, because the dog will eat the cupcakes. What should he do?

5 In pairs or small groups, think of a simple school fair game. Make an advertisement with rules and tips to win.

forty-seven 47

Story lab
READING

I will understand the sequence of a story.

1 Look at the title and the pictures. What do you think the story is about?

2 Read. Put the paragraphs in the correct order. Then listen and check.

THE SCHOOL MUSICAL!

CODE CRACKER

A

"And now for our final performance!" Lily heard Miss Carter say to the audience in the school hall.

"Are you ready?" Lily asked her friends as they waited behind the stage curtains. The curtains opened.

"We are *The Trash Band*!" said Lily. And they began to "play".

Lily was playing a guitar. She made it from a cereal box and some rubber bands. Deniz was blowing on a cardboard tube "trumpet", and Hassan was blowing over a plastic bottle. Leyla was hitting a metal can and Emir was shaking some bottle tops in two paper cups.

B

"Don't forget, everyone!" Miss Carter said. "It's our school musical show next week. We want to sell a lot of tickets so that we can buy some new musical instruments for our school. I hope you are all thinking of something to perform. Remember, you must give me your ideas by the end of the week. Lily, I'm still waiting for your group's idea."

"But nobody in my group can play a musical instrument, Miss Carter," said Lily. "We aren't musical."

"You don't have to be musical," said Miss Carter. "You just have to be entertaining and creative. But it's important to practice first so start thinking!"

C

It was the day before the show. Lily's classmates were all busy practicing. They were writing songs and playing musical instruments. But Lily and her friends still couldn't agree on their performance.

D

"What are we going to do?" said Lily to her friends. "We *must* think of something. The show starts in a few hours!"

Lily looked out of the window. Then she noticed the recycling box outdoors. It was full of old boxes, tubes, and bottles.

"I've got an idea!" she said excitedly.

E

The audience loved it. They cheered and clapped along to the rhythm. It was clear that *The Trash Band* was the most popular act in the show.

"Miss Carter was right," said Lily. "You really don't have to be musical to be entertaining!"

3 Look at the recycling in the story. Circle the trash that Lily's group used.

4 Design and make your own musical instrument, using trash!

Values Fund our school.

5 Think and discuss.

1. What things do schools need to buy?
2. What other ways can you think of to help schools earn money?

6 Think about what other musical instrument you could make from trash. Act out the story in groups.

Experiment lab
MATH: SPENDING AND EARNING MONEY

I will learn about business.

1 Look at the photo and discuss. Do you and your friends buy similar things? How much do they cost?

Watch a video about profit and loss.

2 Read and answer.

1. Who invented this product?
2. How much money did the inventor spend on making the product?
3. Did he earn more or less than he spent?

| HOME | NEWS | FORUM | ARTICLES |

Mr Cheong Choon Ng had two daughters. One day, he watched them as they were making bracelets from rubber bands. He started helping his daughters, but his fingers were too big! So, he designed a board with some pins in it and started weaving the rubber bands in a colorful, diamond-shaped pattern on this "loom". He made several bracelets which the girls took to school the next day.

Suddenly, their dad became a hero! Everyone wanted one of the bracelets. The family decided to start making "loom band kits" which had all the materials to make a loom band. They saved $10,000 and spent it all on rubber bands and the materials to make loom band kits to sell. The girls reviewed the loom bands on the internet, while their dad visited large toy stores to tell them about the product. Each kit cost $15. The first order from a toy store was for 12 loom band kits. The loom band kits became really popular.

In the years that followed, Mr Cheong Choon Ng sold millions of kits and made huge profits.

COMMENT

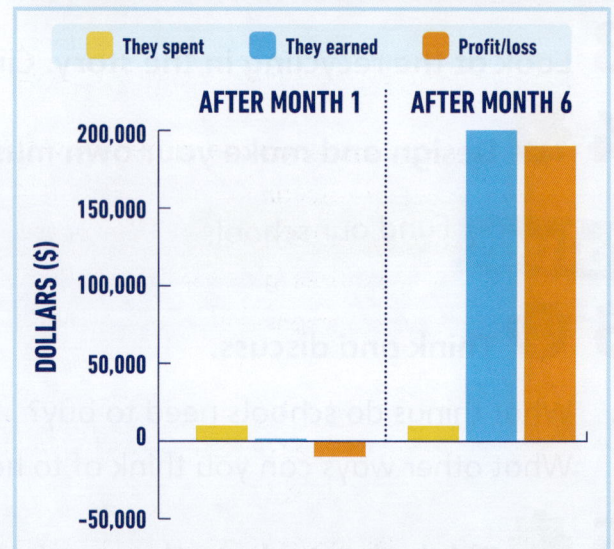

3 Work in pairs and answer.

MATH ZONE

A woman from the UK bought 24,000 rubber bands for £45 and made a dress out of them. She put an advertisement online. She wanted to make a profit of £50.

1. What was the lowest price the woman wanted for the dress?

The woman was shocked when someone offered to pay £170,000 for the dress. In the end that didn't happen and she sold the dress for £220.

2. How much profit did she make?

When you sell something, you have to think carefully about the price. You can make more profit when something costs more, but you might sell fewer products.

One week, Li bought some rubber bands for $5. She made 10 loom bands. She sold the loom bands for $5 each.

3. How much did each loom band cost her to make?
4. How much profit or loss did Li make on each loom band?

Carlo wanted to print and sell T-shirts. He bought 10 T-shirts for $30. He printed a picture on them and sold them at the school fair. The price for each T-shirt was $8. He sold three T-shirts.

5. How much did each T-shirt cost him to make?
6. How much profit or loss did Carlo make?

EXPERIMENT TIME

Calculating profit and loss

Juan wants to sell lemonade at the school fair. A local store gives Juan the ice for free and he doesn't have to pay for the water or the glasses. To make four glasses of lemonade he needs a bag of lemons and a bag of sugar.

	Price for a bag of lemons	Price for a bag of sugar
Mario's grocery store	$2.70	$1.30
SUPER S supermarket	$2.50	$1.35
Farmers' market	$2.75	$1.25

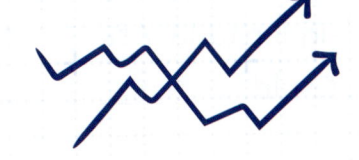

1. Which store should Juan go to for the best prices? How much will he have to spend there in total?
2. Juan sells four glasses of lemonade for $1.25 each. Does he make a profit or a loss? How much?

fifty-one 51

Could you do me a favor?

COMMUNICATION: REQUESTS FOR HELP

I will ask and respond to requests for help.

1 Complete these requests for help.

1. Could you do me a favor and ____ , please?
2. Would you ____ , please?
3. Would you ____ and put them in a box for me, please?
4. Could I ____ ?

a borrow a pen, please
b show me how this works
c open the door for me
d do me a favor

2 🎧 026 Listen and check.

3 💬 Work in pairs. Practice asking and answering polite questions in these situations.

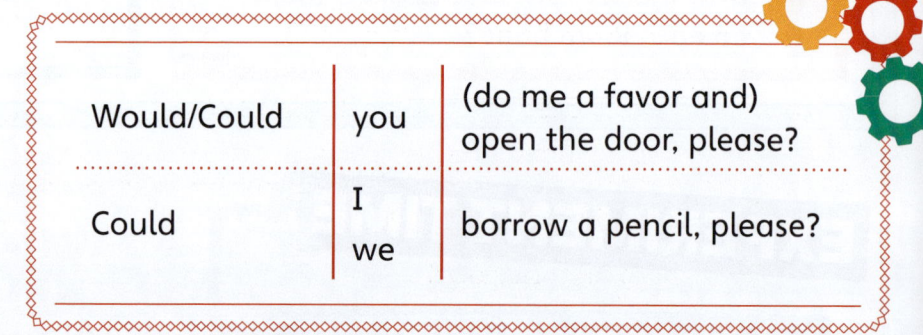

Would/Could	you	(do me a favor and) open the door, please?
Could	I / we	borrow a pencil, please?

1. You are in a café. You want to buy a glass of lemonade but you don't have any money. You would like to borrow some money from a friend.
   Could _____?

2. You don't have a dictionary. Ask your teacher for one.
   Would _____?

3. You want someone to help you reach a book on a high shelf.
   Could _____?

4. You can't read the signs at a station because they are in a language you don't understand. Ask someone to help you.
   Could _____?

Writing lab
WRITING AN ADVERTISEMENT

I will write an advertisement.

1 Look at the advertisement. Where do you think you could see an advertisement like this?

2 Read the advertisement. Find and underline two examples of each feature in the tip box.

> Advertisements use different ways to persuade us to buy a product or service:
> - questions
> - adjectives
> - superlative adjectives
> - facts
> - opinions
> - exclamation marks.

Do you often feel like a QUICK, CHEAP, TASTY SNACK?

ONLY $9.99!

POPCORN IS THE BEST – and you can make it in your own kitchen! With this amazing electric popcorn maker it will only take a few minutes!

- The healthiest popcorn maker you can buy – you don't have to use any oil.
- Easy to use – just turn it on and watch the corn pop!
- New, still in the box.

Everybody loves popcorn! And everybody should have a popcorn maker in their home! So what are you waiting for?
Buy it NOW!

3 Think of a product to advertise to your friends. Include key information, an attractive design, and a picture of the product.

4 Display your advertisements around the classroom. Which of the products would you buy? Why? How did the advertisement persuade you?

fifty-three 53

PROJECT AND REVIEW

Make a video advertisement for your business

Step 1

Research

✈ Find out about the features of written and video advertisements.

- ☐ Check the features of each type of advertisement.
- ☐ Look back at your own written advertisement from Writing lab. Which features did it have?
- ☐ Work in groups. Choose one written advertisement and plan how to change it into a video advertisement.

	Written ads	Video ads
Quick to create	✓	
Easy to make	✓	
Colorful	✓	✓
Key words and features are easy to see		
Essential information in one place		
Sounds and voices		✓
Can tell a story		

Step 2

Plan

✈ Make a plan for your advertisement.

- ☐ Decide what product or service you are going to advertise and think of a name for it.
- ☐ Discuss the information you will include in your video advertisement.
- ☐ Plan the location for filming, music, etc.
- ☐ Decide on roles for each person in your group (actor, narrator, cameraperson, etc.).

WOOF WOOF WALKS!

Whose dogs could we walk?	neighbors' dogs, friends' dogs
Where could we walk them?	the park, the beach
When can we take them there?	the park is open every day, 7:00 a.m.–6:30 p.m.
How long will the walks be?	30–60 minutes

54 fifty-four

Step 3

Create

> 🛩 Design your advertisement and video it.

- ☐ Plan the scenes and script for each part of your advertisement.
- ☐ Use questions to make people think about what they need.
- ☐ Use adjectives and superlatives to describe your product or service.
- ☐ Include facts and opinions.
- ☐ Check your punctuation!
- ☐ Film your advertisement.

The dog is sitting sadly by the door. The owner has gone to work.
Script: Are you busy at work? Is your dog all alone?

Close up of Andrea, speaking to camera.
Script: You need a dog walker! You should call WOOF WOOF WALKS!

Andrea is running in the park with the dog, playing with a ball.
Script: WOOF WOOF will give your dog a wonderful walk!

Step 4

Show and tell

> 🛩 Hold a class competition for the best video advertisement.

- ☐ Show your video advertisement to the class.
- ☐ Your friends will choose the best three.
- ☐ What did they like? What could you do differently or better?

Now I can ...

- ... use words to talk about business and money.
- ... use modals to talk about rules and advice.
- ... ask and respond to requests for help.
- ... write an advertisement.

fifty-five 55

4 Food for the future!

How can I create a sustainable farm for the future?

1 💬 Look and discuss. Would you like to try the food?

GRASSHOPPER · CRICKET · MEALWORM · BUFFALO WORM

SOURCES OF PROTEIN FOR THE FUTURE!

seaweeds and algae ☐   lab-grown burgers ☐

jackfruit ☐   insects ☐

2 💬 What would you eat? Read and number in order for you. Compare and discuss with a partner.

56 fifty-six

3 Read. What have you eaten today?

NUTRIENT GROUPS

CARBOHYDRATE Carbohydrates, including sugar, give our body energy. We find carbohydrate in foods such as bread, pasta, and rice.

PROTEIN We need protein to grow and be strong. Protein is in meat, fish, beans and lentils, and dairy products.

FAT Fat is a source of energy and we need fat to grow and have healthy skin. Fat is found in oils such as olive oil and sunflower oil, and in dairy products such as yogurt and milk.

FIBER Fiber is a type of carbohydrate that we can't digest. It is in fruit, vegetables, and whole grains. It keeps our digestive system healthy.

Food and farming
VOCABULARY

I will learn about food and farming.

1 🎧 027 **Look at the first infographic. Then listen and answer.**

Which foods are the most unhealthy?
a fruit and vegetables
b sugary foods
c meat and fish

2 🎧 028 **Look at the second infographic. Then listen and answer.**

Which type of farming doesn't use pesticides?
a intensive farming
b organic farming
c sustainable farming

- FOOD HIGH IN FAT AND SUGAR — 1 _____
- FATS AND OILS — 2 _____
- MEAT, FISH, EGGS, BEANS, AND NUTS — 3 _____
- DAIRY — 4 _____
- CEREALS, BREAD, POTATOES, PASTA, AND RICE — 5 _____
- FRUIT AND VEGETABLES — 6 _____

Agriculture
- Sustainable farming
- Intensive farming
- Pesticides
- Organic farming
- Pollinator

58 fifty-eight

3 Complete the section on the right of infographic 1.

> 2 servings per day   3 servings per day
> 3–5 servings per day   5+ servings per day
> in small amounts   not every day

4 Listen to Mike talking about his farm. Which farm is his? Check ✓.

a
b
c

5 Listen again. Then read and circle.

1. Mike's farm is intensive / organic / sustainable.
2. The cows on the farm produce milk / meat / honey.
3. Mike's parents use very little grass / pesticide / bees.
4. They have flowers to encourage cows / pollinators / fruit trees.

Values Food sustainability.

6 Read and discuss.

1. Where does the food you eat come from?
2. Which foods that you eat come from your country and which come from other countries?
3. Why do you think it is important for farms to be sustainable?
4. Why do you think we need pollinators?

7 Circle the words with an *aw* sound in red, and the words with an *oo* sound in blue. Then listen and check your answers.

August   blue   caught
drew   flew   flute
June   saw
thought   true

fifty-nine 59

Language lab

GRAMMAR 1: TALKING ABOUT THE FUTURE

I will learn how to talk about the future.

1 Watch the video.

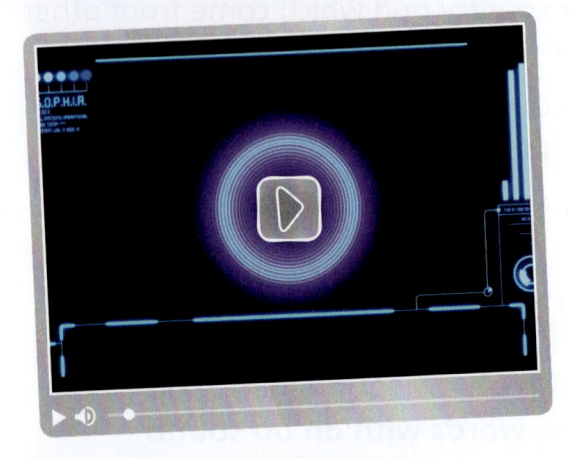

will

Predictions → It **will** rain tomorrow.

Decisions made in the moment → "The market closes in an hour." "Really? I'**ll** go now."

going to

Predictions → It's **going to** be delicious!

Intentions → I'm **going to** eat less sugar.

Present Progressive

Definite plans → I'**m visiting** an organic farm on Saturday.

2 Look, read and circle.

1. What are you going to do for your project?
   We're going to research sustainable farming.

   prediction   intention

2. I forgot to feed the chickens!
   Don't worry, I'll do it for you.

   decision made in the moment   plan

3. Bees are going to die out in the future.
   There won't be anything to pollinate all the fruit and vegetables we eat.

   prediction   intention

4. What are you doing on the weekend?
   We're picking olives on our uncle's farm on Saturday.

   decision made in the moment   plan

3 Read and complete with the words below.

THE FUTURE OF FOOD AND FARMING

What **1** _____ you having for dinner tonight? I'm **2** _____ meat and vegetables. However, what we eat in the future, **3** _____ probably be different because scientists think that farming methods **4** _____ be different. They predict that humans will have to find alternative sources of protein because intensive farming **5** _____ be sustainable. Farming animals for meat contributes to global warming. So, what other types of protein are we **6** _____ to eat? Scientists think we are **7** _____ to eat more plant proteins and even things like algae from the ocean, insects, and worms! **8** _____ you give insects a try?

1	a	will	b	are	c	going
2	a	having	b	going	c	have
3	a	will	b	not	c	to
4	a	going	b	will	c	are
5	a	don't	b	isn't	c	won't
6	a	going	b	will	c	not
7	a	do	b	going	c	will
8	a	Are	b	Will	c	Do

4 Read and write.

1 Make a prediction about a friend's lunch.   _____
2 Write a good intention about the food you eat.   _____
3 Write a plan you have for the weekend.   _____
4 Make a decision in the moment.   _____

5 Play *Future Game* in groups.

- Play in groups of four.
- Spin a spinner to move around the board.
- Speak about the topics using the correct future form.
- On the question word squares ask someone a question about the future.
- The first player to the finish wins.

Story lab
READING

I will read a science-fiction story.

1 Look at the pictures. Do you think this story is set in the past, present, or future?

2 Read and listen. Check your answer to **1**.

The tiny robots

The huge greenhouses were Fatima's favorite place. Since Fatima and her family moved to the Mars colony a year ago, she spent most of her free time there among the plants and trees. It was the place on the colony that reminded her most of planet Earth. It even had a fake blue sky with clouds which went dark at night and had sunlight during the day! Fatima enjoyed watching the agriculture robots working hard to produce enough fresh food to feed the colony. She felt proud as she watched the robots plant, cultivate, and water the plants because her dad designed and built them.

The human gardeners, however, were getting more and more worried every time she went.

One day, she asked the head gardener, Iris, why everyone was so worried.

"It's all our fruit and vegetable crops, Fatima," she answered. "Look – they aren't flowering. That means they are failing. I don't understand because everything is sustainable."

3 Read the text again and circle T (True) or F (False).

1. Fatima lives on planet Earth. — T / F
2. Fatima is proud of the human gardeners. — T / F
3. The fruits and vegetables are an important source of fiber. — T / F
4. There aren't any bugs or insects in the greenhouse. — T / F
5. Fatima's dad won't make the small robots. — T / F
6. Fatima's idea saves the harvest. — T / F

"Are the plants getting enough light and water?" asked Fatima.

"Absolutely," replied Iris. "The robots make sure that every plant has all the water and nutrients it needs. Your dad's inventions mean that sunlight is intensified to the correct levels for the Earth plants. We need the fruit and vegetables because they are an important source of fiber, protein, and vitamins. We have stores of food from Earth, but we need to grow our own."

"What will happen?" asked Fatima.

"I don't know," said Iris, sadly, "but we are going to run out of food in six months."

"Maybe it's pesticides," suggested Fatima.

"No, it can't be," Iris replied. "Everything is organic here. There are no bugs or insects, so we don't use pesticides."

Fatima suddenly had an idea. She ran as quickly as she could to her dad's workshop.

"Dad!" she said, out of breath from running. "You can make any robot. Can you design a lot of tiny ones?" She explained what was happening in the greenhouses and told him her idea.

"I'll try!" he said.

Six months later, the plants in the greenhouses were full of fruit and vegetables. The agriculture robots were working hard to collect the harvest. All around them, thousands of other tiny robots were busy working. These were the bee robots that were Fatima's idea. They were busy pollinating the plants for the next season's harvest.

4 Make your own pipe cleaner bees.

- Twist black and yellow pipe cleaners together to create a stripy bee body.
- Make wing shapes with white pipe cleaners and stick them on your bee body.

5 Act out the story in groups.

sixty-three 63

Experiment lab
SCIENCE: FOOD CHAINS

I will learn about food chains.

1 Look at the plants and animals. Which organism gets its energy from the sun? Check ✓.

Watch a video about food chains.

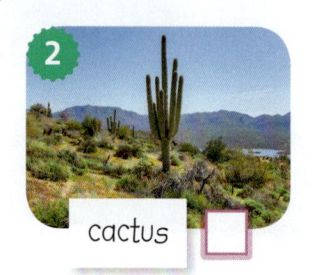

1. snake ☐
2. cactus ☐
3. hawk ☐
4. mouse ☐

_____ _____ _____ _____

2 Read and listen. Where are humans in their food chains?

FOOD CHAINS

A food chain shows how living things get food in their ecosystem, and how nutrients and energy are passed from each living thing. Look at this simple forest food chain.

Producer → Primary consumer → Secondary consumer → Tertiary consumer

PRODUCER
Plants take energy from the sun and turn it into nutrients.

PRIMARY CONSUMER
These are small creatures, such as insects or rabbits, that eat plants. Plant-eating animals are called herbivores.

SECONDARY CONSUMER
These animals could be omnivores (something that eats plants and animals) like small birds or rats, or they could be small carnivores like snakes.

TERTIARY CONSUMER
These are usually carnivores. Carnivores eat other animals. Some food chains have a fourth consumer at the top called a **quaternary consumer**.

It's not just plants and wild animals that are part of food chains. Humans are at the top of their food chains! Humans are naturally omnivores; however, some people choose not to eat meat. Vegetarians don't eat meat, but eat animal products like dairy and eggs, and vegans don't eat meat or any animal products.

3. **Complete the number lines. Then add more numbers to lines 3 and 4.**

fortieth   four
fourth   quaternary

MATH ZONE

1	one	two	three	_____
2	primary	secondary	tertiary	_____
3	first	second	third	_____ _____ _____
4	tenth	twentieth	thirtieth	_____ _____ _____

4. **Read the text again. Label the organisms in 1.**

CODE CRACKER

primary consumer   secondary consumer   tertiary consumer
        producer

EXPERIMENT TIME

How does energy pass through an ocean food chain?

cod   krill   seal
orca   plankton

1. Look at the ocean creatures. Put the name of each organism on a paper cup. Research the ocean food chain and put the cups in order. Then draw a line on each cup to show how much energy that creature needs.

2. Find out how the sun's energy moves through the food chain.
   - Place the paper cups on a tray, in order, and about 3 cm apart.
   - Put 1 liter of water in a bowl at the beginning of the food chain. This is the sun.
   - Use a plant pot to transfer the energy through the food chain.
   - Make predictions. Try it out!

How long will it take to fill the last cup all the way to the line? Where does the lost energy go?

sixty-five 65

It might rain!

COMMUNICATION: *MIGHT* AND *WILL*

I will talk about future possibilities.

We **might** grow food in laboratories in the future.
He's a vegan so he **might not** eat anything on the menu.

> Remember we use *will/won't* for more certain predictions about the future.

1 Look at the weather forecast. Read and circle.

DAY	WEATHER	PROBABILITY
Monday	☀️	35%
	🌧️	50%
Tuesday	☀️	100%
	🌧️	0%
Wednesday	☀️	0%
	🌧️	60%

1. On Monday it might / will be sunny.
2. It might / won't rain on Monday.
3. It won't / might not rain on Tuesday.
4. It might / will be sunny on Tuesday.
5. On Wednesday it might not / won't be sunny.
6. It might not / won't rain on Wednesday.

2 Think and answer. Discuss with a partner.

CODE CRACKER

The farmer wants to plant her corn. She needs two dry days to plant it, but the ground can be wet. It's good for the new crops if it rains the next day. Look at the weather forecast and the additional information on the right. When should she plant the corn?

> It might not be sunny on Sunday, but it won't rain.
>
> It might not be dry on Thursday.

3 Write possibilities for your weekend. Discuss with a partner.

This weekend I might _____
_____.

I might not _____.

Writing lab

WRITING ABOUT AN EVENT IN A NEWSLETTER

I will write a newsletter entry.

1 Look quickly at the text. What does SOFM stand for?

SUSTAINABLE AND ORGANIC FOOD MARKET

After the success of last year's **Sustainable and Organic Food Market** (SOFM), this year's SOFM, on **Wednesday, April 3rd**, will be bigger and better!

STALLS WILL INCLUDE:
- **Mick's Organics.** The fruit and vegetables are grown organically in the owner's garden!
- **Yumi's Honey.** Enjoy nature's sweet treat with honey from Yumi's own bee hives.
- **Bread from Cornfield Bakery.** Includes organic, artisan, and gluten-free loaves.

THERE WILL ALSO BE A LOT OF CAFÉS SERVING FOOD-TO-GO. THESE INCLUDE:
- **The Vegan Kitchen.** Burgers, sandwiches, and wraps, all free from animal products.
- **The Bug Café.** That's right – bugs! Give them a try – insects are a tasty, sustainable source of protein!

Come along and raise money to fund our vegetable garden project!
STALLS AND CAFÉS WILL BE OPEN 3:00 P.M.–7:00 P.M.

2 Read again. Write the name of the stall or café where you can buy these things.

1. _____ 2. _____ 3. _____

3 Plan an event with a partner. Then write your newsletter entry.

4 Draw pictures or find photos to decorate your newsletter entry. Present it to the class.

- Use future tenses for a future event.
- Use bold to make important information stand out.
- Use bullet points to create a list.

sixty-seven 67

PROJECT AND REVIEW

Create a 3D plan of a sustainable farm for the future

Step 1

Research

▷ Decide what food to produce.

- ☐ List the foods you'd like to produce and their main nutrients.
- ☐ Compare your list with other students.
- ☐ Get into groups with students who want to produce the same food.
- ☐ Research different types of sustainable farming.

Vegetables (fiber, carbohydrate)

Dairy (protein, minerals)

I'm going to plan a farm which produces vegetables and dairy products.

I'm going to produce vegetables, too, but I might not produce any animal products.

Step 2

Plan

▷ Decide how to make your farm sustainable.

- ☐ Discuss how you are going to make your farm sustainable for the future.
- ☐ Make sketches of different parts of your farm on sticky notes.
- ☐ Arrange the sticky notes to plan the layout of your farm.

We're going to have flowers growing around our fruit trees for pollinators.

We're going to catch big insects for food.

Don't cut down any trees – keep them on the farm.

68 sixty-eight

Step 3
Create

> Create your model farm.

- [ ] Decide which materials you are going to use for your farm.
- [ ] Create your model farm.
- [ ] Think about how your farm might change over the years. Write your ideas.

clay

tissue paper

cardboard

sponge

popsicle sticks

Create a small sustainable vegetable garden at home. You can create it outside, or in some pots.

Step 4
Show and tell

> Present your farm to the class.

- [ ] Invite other groups to visit your farm.
- [ ] Present your farm and talk about your plans for it.

> This is our farm. We're going to produce food from all the main nutrient groups: protein from eggs; carbohydrate from potatoes; fiber from apples; and fat from milk. We're going to be sustainable by having lots of trees and we'll plant new things every year.

Now I can ...

- ... use words to talk about food and farming.
- ... use the correct future form.
- ... use *might* to talk about future possibilities.
- ... write a newsletter entry.

sixty-nine 69

2 Checkpoint
UNITS 3 AND 4

1 🎧 033 **Listen and complete the quiz for Vaun. What should Vaun continue doing in the future?**

How do you feel about THE FUTURE OF FOOD?

1 Which statement do you agree with most?
- A We mustn't eat meat or animal products.
- B You have to eat meat or fish to get enough protein.
- C We must stop using pesticides.

2 What changes are you going to make to your diet in the future?
- A I'm going to eat more lab-grown burgers and insects.
- B None! I have a balanced diet. Why should I change anything?
- C I'm going to eat more organic food.

3 Which of these products do you think could be good business ideas?
- A Recycle your plastic bottles in the garden!
- B Save money – make your own candy in our sugar-free candy machine!
- C Help the bees. Put a sustainable bee hotel in your back yard!

4 Which of these do you think we will need more of in the future?
- A Insects. They're going to be the new superfood!
- B Algae. It's cheap, easy to find, and full of protein!
- C Bees. Without them, we'll run out of ALL types of food.

5 Do you ever spend money on a product after you see an advertisement for it?
- A No, I don't have a lot of money.
- B Yes, but the price has to be right.
- C No, we should recycle more and stop buying new things.

6 Which prediction do you agree with most?
- A There won't be any cows on farms.
- B We'll invent a single food that will give us all the nutrients we need.
- C All schools will have greenhouses in their school yards.

NOW FIND OUT YOUR RESULTS!

Mostly As It's good to see that you care about food and the environment. You don't have to avoid meat, but it's true that eating less of it will help. That's something we should all be doing.

Mostly Bs The world is going to change. You might have to consider different ways of living in the future. Use your creative business skills to invent a product to help food production in the future!

Mostly Cs You think a lot about the environment. Keep up the good work! Don't give up your campaigns to save the environment! Thanks to people like you we can be positive about the future.

70 seventy

2 Read about Vaun's business idea. Answer the questions.

HELP THE BEES – BUY A BEE HOTEL!

Bees have lost a large part of their natural habitat over the last 60 years. But you can help them by buying a BEE HOTEL!

In our simple bee hotel we use only recycled and sustainable materials – an old plastic bottle filled with bamboo. It's cheap and easy to make, too.

- All you need is a dry area outdoors.
- The bee hotel must be about a meter off the ground.
- And you don't need a backyard. All the bees need is a few flowers growing in a pot and some water.

Hang up your bee hotel and watch them move in! The bees will lay their eggs in the bamboo and use the pollen from your flowers to feed their young.

So what are you waiting for?

BEE helpful, BEE kind to the environment – and buy a BEE hotel!

1. Find at least one fact in the advertisement.
2. Find two opinion adjectives.
3. What two conditions are necessary for the location of a bee hotel?
4. What two natural resources does the owner of a bee hotel have to provide?

3 Which picture, a, b, or c, follows the correct instructions for using the bee hotel?

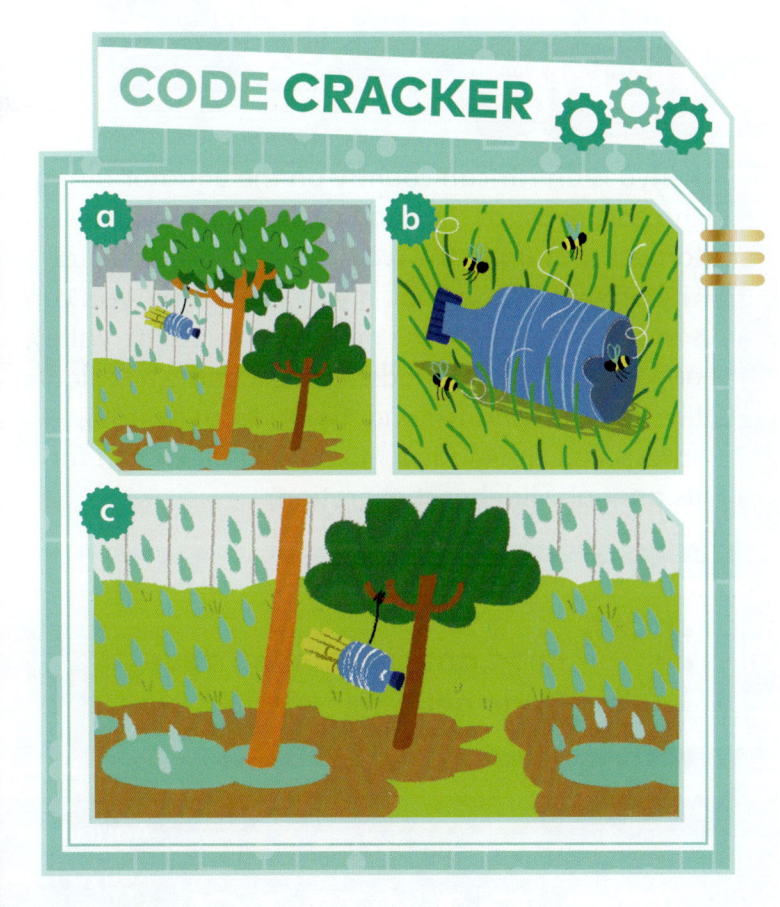

CODE CRACKER

4 Work in pairs. Write an advertisement for a "green" home-made product.

Include information about:
- how it will help the environment
- why it isn't harmful to the environment
- how cheap and easy it is to make
- what recycled materials it consists of.

5 Look back at the quiz. Ask and answer with a partner. Find out how many of your classmates have the same results as you.

Test your progress with English Benchmark Young Learners

Kenya
CULTURE

KENYA

Kenya is an African country on the equator along the east coast of the continent. It is the 48th largest country in the world by area. The capital city of Kenya is Nairobi. If you visit Kenya, you can see savanna, lakes, the dramatic Great Rift Valley, and mountain highlands. It's also home to wildlife like lions, elephants, and rhinos. From Nairobi, safaris visit the Maasai Mara Reserve, known for its annual wildebeest migration.

Fun Fact!

There are more than 60 languages spoken in Kenya, and more than 40 ethnic groups. Almost everyone in Kenya speaks more than one language!

1 Read and listen. Who does Fair Trade help?

FAIR TRADE FARMING

Agriculture and farming is one of Kenya's biggest exports. Kenya is one of the main producers of the world's two favorite hot drinks, coffee and tea. The farmers also grow something that many people enjoy – flowers!

Kenya is one of many countries around the world which benefits from a global trade initiative called Fair Trade. Fair Trade is about better prices, good working conditions, local sustainability, and fair terms of trade for farmers and workers in the developing world. Fair Trade means that anyone who buys the produce must pay sustainable prices. The prices are controlled so they never fall lower than the market price. This means that the farmers can make a profit from the food and produce they grow, and invest in their farms. This allows them to improve and make their farms more sustainable, which will make their farms more productive and more profitable.

With Fair Trade you have the power to change the world every time you visit the grocery store. As well as coffee, tea, and flowers, you can also buy Fair Trade bananas and chocolate, and clothes made from Fair Trade cotton.

Last year, Fair Trade USA empowered more than 900,000 farmers in 45 countries around the world to reach better terms with their trading partners. Look out for the Fair Trade logo on the products you buy and know that you'll be helping farmers and farm workers in countries like Kenya.

2 Read again and answer.

1. What six Fair Trade products are mentioned in the text?
   _____ _____ _____ _____ _____ _____

2. Which of the products are grown in Kenya according to the text?
   _____ _____ _____

3. Circle all the words that apply: Fair Trade makes farms more …

   profitable   organic   intensive   sustainable

3 Read and discuss.

1. Is there a Fair Trade initiative in your country?
2. Do you buy any Fair Trade products?
3. Why are initiatives like Fair Trade so important for farmers?

4 Listen. What does the Victorious Craft Group make?

5 Make jewelry from recycled trash. Present your jewelry to the class.

My Culture

6 Read and discuss.

1. What traditional arts and crafts are made in your country?
2. Where can you buy traditional items?
3. Draw a picture of your favorite traditional craft object from your country.

Maria doll – Mexico

seventy-three 73

5 The ancient world

How can I make an audio tour guide about the past?

1 Look and discuss.

1. Where are the children?
2. What are they going to learn about?
3. Would you like to visit this place? Why/Why not?

2 How much do you know about ancient Egypt? Work in pairs and do the quiz. Then listen and check your answers.

1. Ancient Egyptians preserved the bodies of … when they died.
   ☐ humans   ☐ humans and animals

2. They put the body in a … made of wood or stone.
   ☐ coffin   ☐ mummy

3. Ancient Egyptian writing is called … .
   ☐ papyrus   ☐ hieroglyphics

3 Write like an Egyptian!

1. On a piece of paper, spell your name in hieroglyphics.
2. Give it your name to the teacher.
3. Take one of the collected pieces of paper and read it. Whose name is written there?

Values Our history.

4 Think and discuss.

1. Is it important to know about the past? Why/Why not?
2. What can we learn from studying ancient worlds?

Ancient Egypt
VOCABULARY

I will learn words to describe life in ancient Egypt.

1 Read, listen, and label the pictures.

coffin   hieroglyphics   papyrus   pyramid   treasure

EGYPTIAN WRITING
- Egyptian writing – **hieroglyphics** – consists of small pictures.
- The Egyptians made paper from drying and weaving the leaves of the **papyrus** plant.

EGYPTIAN RULERS
- The ancient Egyptians built **pyramids** as **burial places** for their kings and queens, also called pharaohs.
- Tutankhamun, the "Boy King", became pharaoh at the age of nine.
- The **archeologist** Howard Carter was amazed when he was **digging** a **hole** and found the **coffin** of King Tut. The coffin contained his **mummy**. They also discovered about 5,000 objects of **treasure**: statues, gold jewelry, model boats, chairs, and paintings.

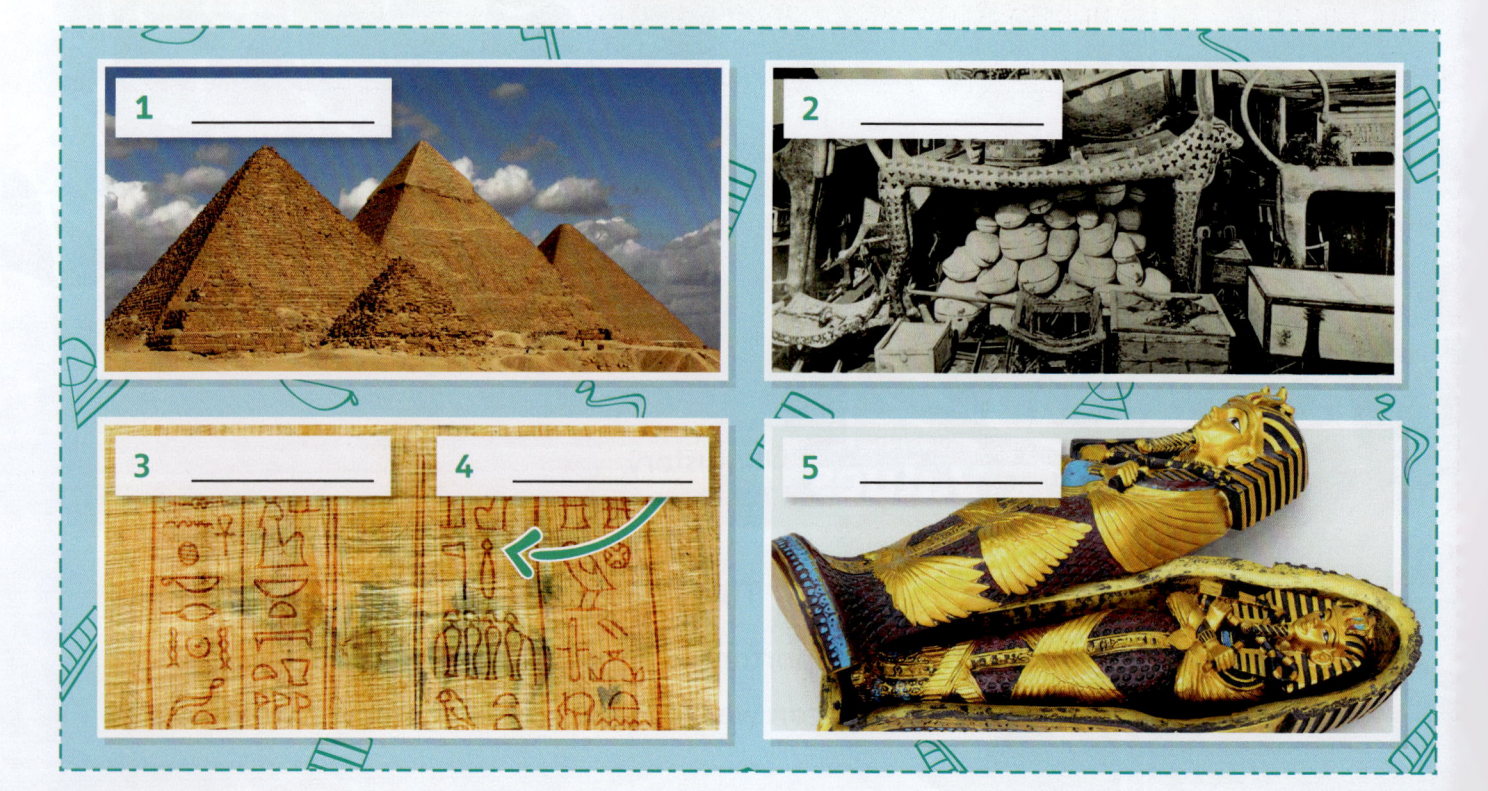

1 _____
2 _____
3 _____
4 _____
5 _____

2 Answer the questions.

1. What did ancient Egyptians use pyramids for?
   _____
2. How did the archeologist find King Tut's mummy and treasure?
   _____

3 Write sentences with the color words from 1.

4 Listen and circle T (True) or F (False).

1. King Tut is called the "Boy King" because he was a boy when he became king.   T / F
2. Nobody found his burial place for about 3,000 years.   T / F
3. The outside of his coffin was covered in gold.   T / F
4. Like all other pharaohs, his burial place was a pyramid.   T / F
5. A British archeologist found the burial place in 1920.   T / F
6. Along with King Tut's mummy, archeologists found about 500 precious objects of treasure.   T / F

5 Read and complete. Then discuss.

The treasure that archeologists found with King Tutankhamun's mummy tells us what was important to people at that time. What objects of "treasure" will tell people in the future about what is important to children of your age, today? Make a list.

a cell phone,   _a soccer team's flag,_   _____   _____   _____

6 Listen to how we say the colored parts of these words. Listen again and repeat.

Can you w**or**k out what this w**or**d means?

Wh**ere**'s the treasure? I'm sure it's over th**ere**!

7 Listen. What sound does each word have? Write 1 or 2. Then listen again and check.

Sound 1	Sound 2
w**or**k	wh**ere**, b**ear**

curtain ___   somewhere ___
hurt ___   fur ___
wear ___   burn ___
pear ___   share ___

Language lab

GRAMMAR 1: PAST PASSIVE

I will learn about the Past Passive.

1 Watch the video.

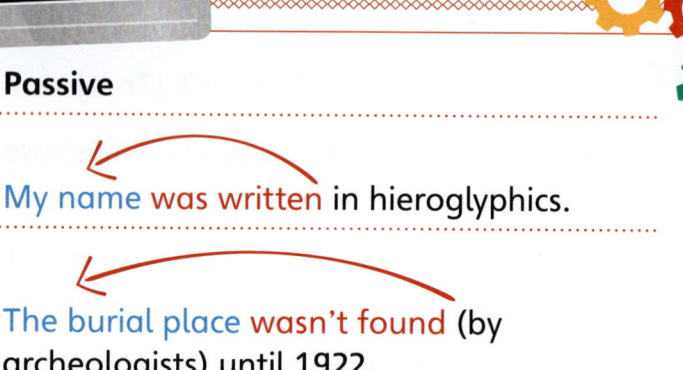

Active	Passive
I wrote my name in hieroglyphics.	My name was written in hieroglyphics.
Archeologists didn't find the burial place until 1922.	The burial place wasn't found (by archeologists) until 1922.
Tourists visited the pyramids.	The pyramids were visited (by tourists).
They published many books about Egypt.	Many books about Egypt were published.

2 Complete the text with the verbs in brackets.

Papyrus is a plant that **1** _was grown_ (grow) beside the River Nile. The roots **2** _____ (eat) and the leaves **3** _____ (use) by ancient Egyptians to make paper. This is how paper **4** _____ (make).

First, the hard outer leaves **5** _____ (remove) and the soft insides **6** _____ (cut) into strips. They **7** _____ (put) in water for three days to soften.

Then the strips **8** _____ (roll) flat and they **9** _____ (lay) next to each other in rows, one row on top of the other.

A heavy stone **10** _____ (place) on the papyrus for a few days. The natural "sugar" in the leaves helped to stick the strips together, like glue. After a few days, the papyrus was dry and ready to use.

3 Number the pictures in order.

CODE CRACKER

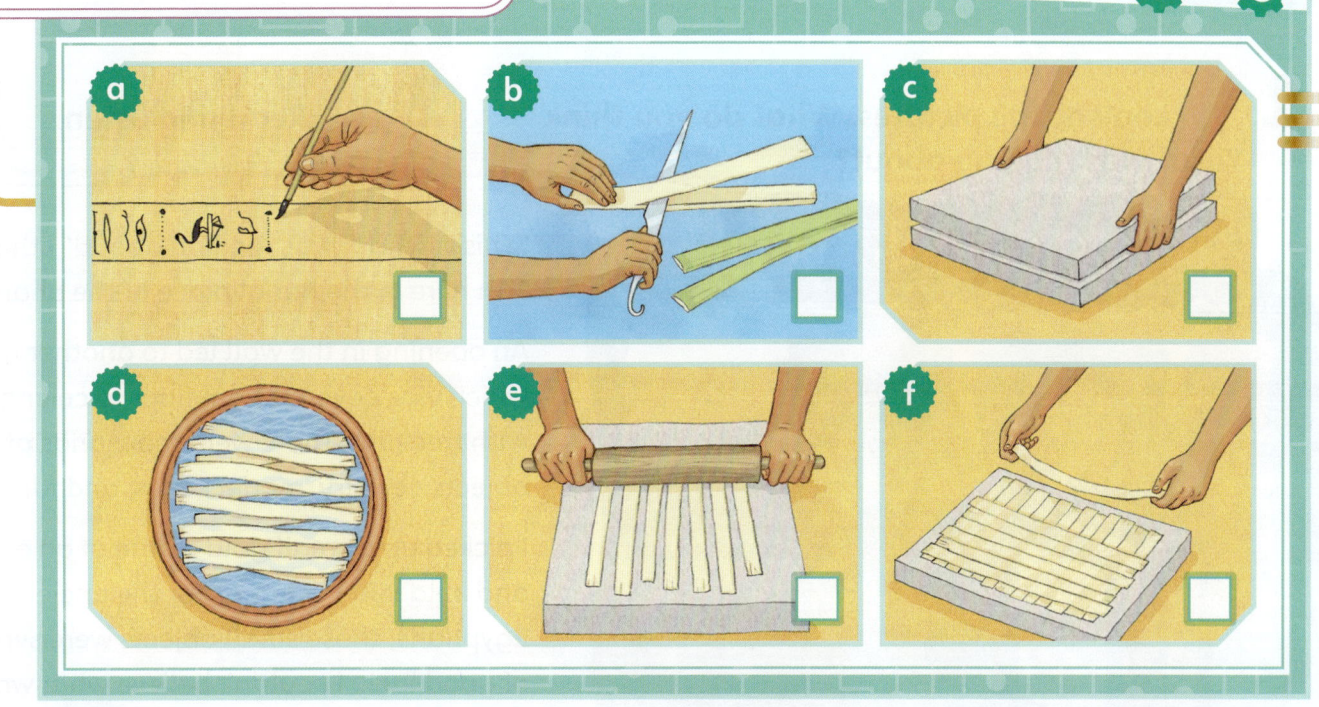

a b c
d e f

4 🎧 041 💬 Work in pairs. Complete and circle. Then listen and check.

1. Chess _____ (invent) 1,500 years ago by the Egyptians / Chinese .

2. The first coins _____ (use) in 200 / 600 BCE.

3. The oldest mummies _____ (find) in Egypt / South America .

4. The first toothpaste _____ (make) by the ancient Greeks / Egyptians , using salt, pepper, and dried flowers.

5. In the ancient world, more pyramids _____ (build) in Sudan / Guatemala than in Egypt.

5 Make your own papyrus!

seventy-nine 79

Story lab
READING

> I will read a story about a boy and his dream.

1 Look at the pictures. What do you think Yusuf was reading about?

2 Read and listen.

A good night story

"Turn off your light, Yusuf!" I heard my mom call from downstairs.

"Yes, Mom, in a minute!" I said. But I couldn't stop reading my book. It was so exciting! It was a true story of how King Tutankhamun's treasures were found by an archeologist. I was at the part where he was at the bottom of some stairs. There was a door in front of him ... What was behind it? I wanted to know what would happen when he opened it.

But ... why was it suddenly so dark? It was impossible to see in front of me. Luckily, I had a flashlight in my pocket. I turned it on and looked around me.

I was at the bottom of some stairs, deep under the ground! "How strange," I thought. "How did I get here? I don't remember walking down here and opening this small door."

I could see a small room, and through that, another room, where paintings on the walls showed ancient Egyptian scenes and hieroglyphics.

"This is what I was reading about!" I thought. "I'm here in the burial place of the pharaoh!"

An opening in the wall led to another room which was covered from floor to ceiling with treasure. There were thousands of gold objects, jewelry, model boats, and furniture.

I picked up a small gold statue of an eagle and held it in my hand. For the ancient Egyptians, these small objects were symbols of good luck. I couldn't believe what was happening to me. I was in the past ... 3,000 years ago!

The next thing I heard was my mom's voice.

"Wake up, Yusuf!" She was shaking me gently as she took my book out of my hands. She opened the curtains and the sunlight came into the room. "You fell asleep while you were reading last night!"

"So that's what happened," I thought. I felt a little disappointed. So I wasn't in the pharaoh's burial place at all!

"I had the most amazing dream," I said to my mom, "but it felt so real ... !"

"Dreams often feel real," she smiled. "Oh, what's this? I've never seen it before." She picked up an object on my bedside table and gave it to me.

It was a small gold statue of an eagle ...

3 Answer the questions.

1. What was Yusuf reading about?
2. Why couldn't he stop reading and go to sleep?
3. Where was he when he put on his flashlight?
4. What treasure did he see in one of the rooms?
5. Why did Yusuf feel disappointed the next morning?

4 Work in pairs. How do you think the statue got on the bedside table?

5 Work in pairs.

Student A: You are Yusuf. Tell your partner about your "dream".

Student B: You are Yusuf's friend. Ask questions to find out more about the "dream".

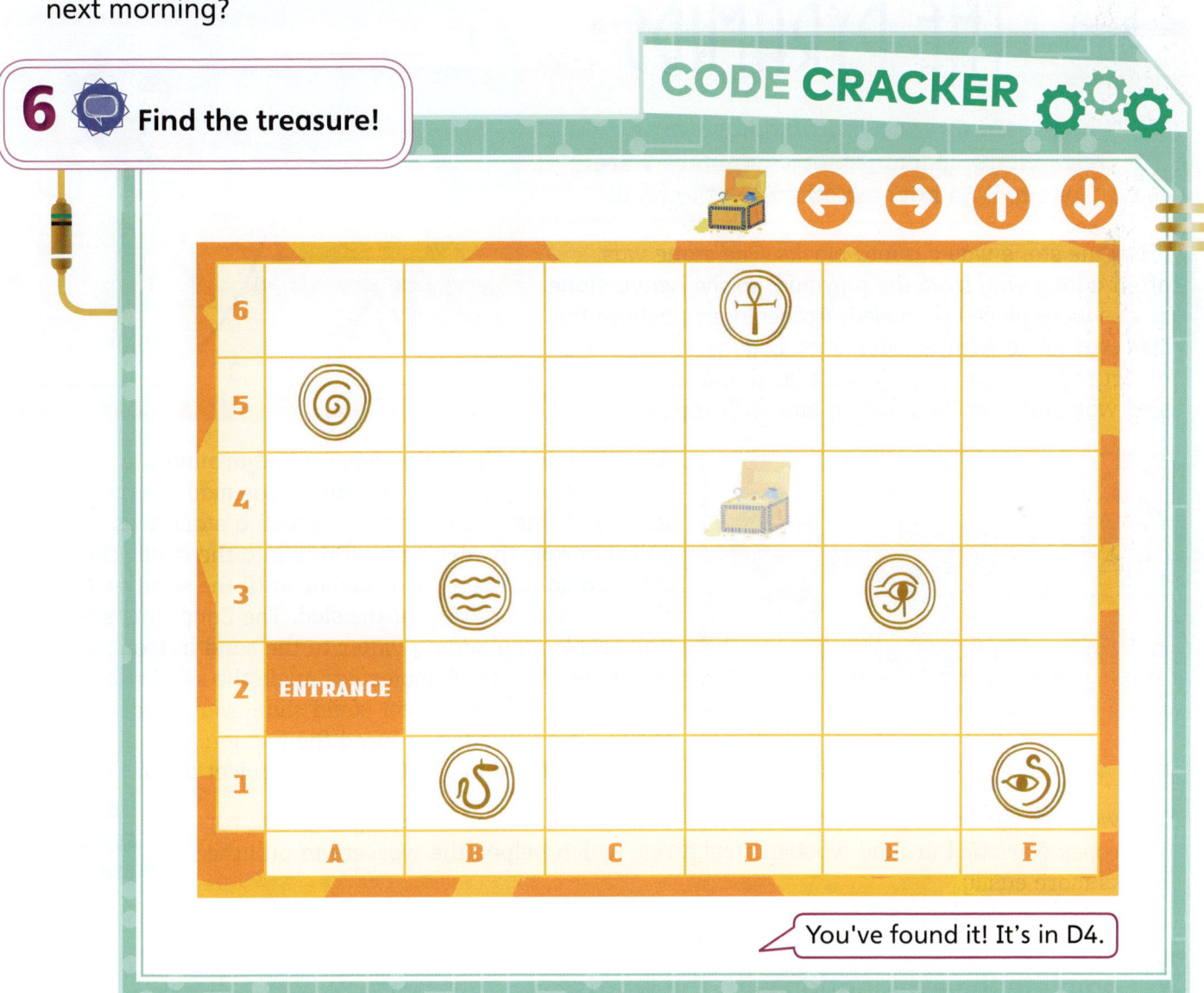

6 Find the treasure!

CODE CRACKER

You've found it! It's in D4.

7 Design your own good luck symbol. Describe it to a partner.

It's made of …

Experiment lab

ENGINEERING: HOW THE PYRAMIDS WERE BUILT

I will learn about force and friction.

1 Look, think, and discuss. How did the ancient Egyptians move the stones to build the pyramids? Label the picture.

log   rope   sled

Watch a video about force and friction.

2 Read.

THE PYRAMIDS

The pyramids were built long before electricity, machines, or computers were invented. So how exactly were they built?

First, the stone was cut into blocks. The stone was often a long way from the pyramid, so the heavy stone blocks were placed on a sled. Archeologists believe the sled was made with wooden logs. Logs were a good object to roll because they were hard and round. The sled was pulled to the building site with ropes.

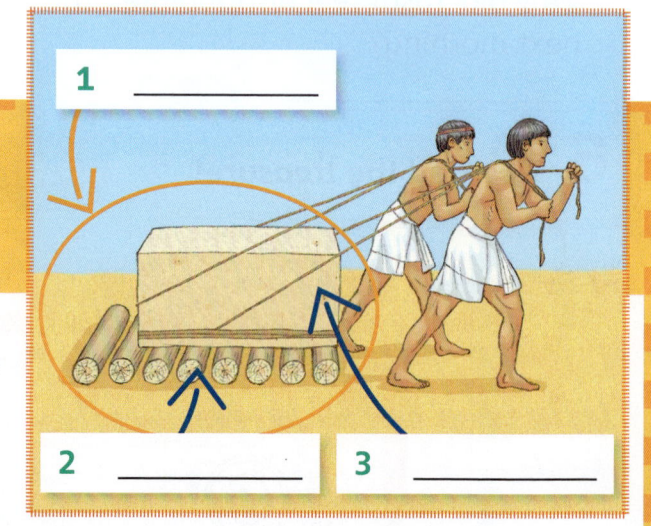

A ramp was built all the way up and around the outside of the pyramid. The ramp was made of rough sand, and this caused friction. When a stone was pulled across the dry sand, it dug into the sand. The stone could not be pulled further until the sand was cleared from the front of the sled. The Egyptians solved this problem by adding water to the sand in front of the stone. The water molecules made the sand stick together so that an object could slide over it more easily. This wet sand reduced the friction, and also halved the force needed to pull the object along.

The workers used stairs on each side of the ramp and pulled the sled up with the ropes. The ropes were tied around wooden structures, which helped the workers to pull the blocks more easily.

3 Complete the explanation with the words.

a force   a ramp   friction

1 _____ is a push or a pull to make an object move in a certain direction. To move an object along a flat surface, from a low level to a higher level, we use 2 _____ . When the object moves along a surface, it causes 3 _____ .

4 Look at the pictures and answer.

1. Which ramp, a or b, needs more force to pull the block, but takes less time?
2. Which ramp needs less force to pull the block, but takes longer?
3. What difference would there be to the force needed to pull the block if the sand was dry or wet?

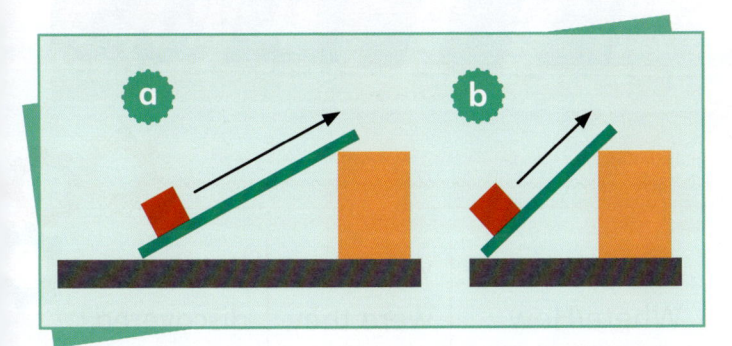

5 What are the missing numbers? Add each pair of blocks together to find out the number that appears in the block above them.

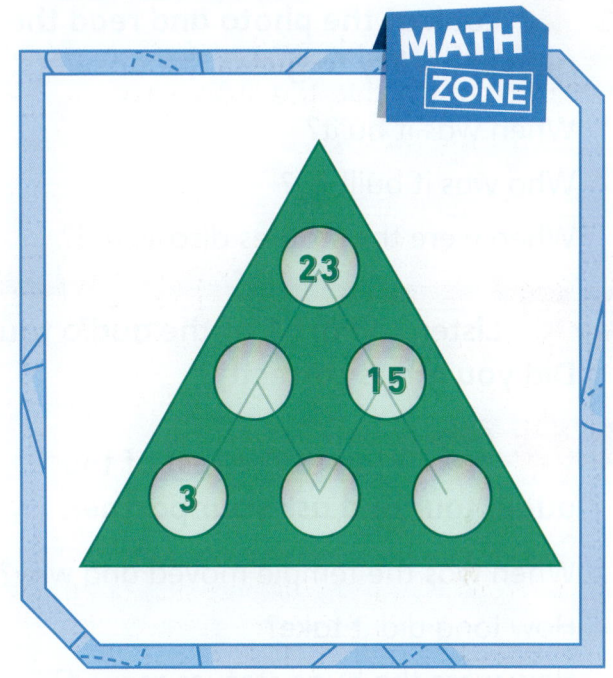

MATH ZONE

23

15

3

EXPERIMENT TIME

How do different surfaces affect friction?

1. Build a ramp to slide or push an object up the surface. Make predictions and write them in your notebook.
   - What difference do you think the size, shape, weight and texture of the object will make?
   - How fast will it move without a lot of force?
   - What difference will the surface make?
   - Will an object need more/less force to move along a smooth/rough surface?
   - What will happen if you pull the object up dry/wet sand?
2. Do the experiment. Were your predictions correct?

Materials

lengths of different materials (smooth and rough)
small objects of different shapes, weights, and textures (smooth and rough)
sand and water

eighty-three 83

A tour back in time
COMMUNICATION: PAST PASSIVE QUESTIONS

I will talk about the history of a place.

1 Look at the photo and read the questions. Try to guess the answers.

1. When was it built?
2. Who was it built by?
3. When were the statues discovered?

2 🎧 043 Listen to Part 1 of the audio tour. Did you guess correctly?

3 🎧 044 💬 Listen to the rest of the audio tour and ask your partner.

1. When was the temple moved and why?
2. How long did it take?
3. How were the huge statues moved?

When/Why/ Where/How	was it were they	built? discovered?
Was Were	it they	moved?
Yes, it/they No, it/they	was/were. wasn't/weren't.	

4 🎧 045 💬 Write the questions. Work in pairs and circle the correct answer. Then listen and check.

1. The Sagrada Familia in Barcelona was designed by (Antoni Gaudí / Oscar Niemeyer).
   Who was the Sagrada Familia in Barcelona designed by?
2. The British Museum was opened in (1957 / 1759).
   _____?
3. The Tower of London was used as a (prison / stadium).
   _____?
4. Make up (was / wasn't) invented by the Egyptians. (Yes, it was. / No, it wasn't).
   _____?

5 💬 Write three questions about a place that you would like to know more about. Then work in pairs and look up the answers.

Who was *the Eiffel Tower* designed by?   When was it first opened?

Writing lab
WRITING A FACT FILE

I will write a fact file.

1 Read the questions. Then find the answers in the fact file.

1. Why were sphinxes built?
2. How big is the Great Sphinx?
3. When was it built?
4. How was it damaged by weather?
5. How was it different in the past?

THE GREAT SPHINX

- Sphinxes were built to guard the entrance to an important place, for example, a pyramid or burial place.
- The most famous sphinx is the Great Sphinx of Giza. It is one of the largest and oldest statues in the world. It is 73 m long and 20 m high. It has the body of a lion and the head of Pharaoh Khafre.
- It was built in about 2500 BCE.
- The Great Sphinx has been badly damaged by weather over the past 4,500 years. The wind has removed its beard, nose, and paint. Archeologists think that the face and body were painted red, the beard was blue, and a lot of the head covering was yellow. No one is sure exactly what color the nose was.

2 In the fact file underline at least one example of:
- a description
- facts about how, when, why, and who
- important dates and what happened
- surprising facts.

- Include a title.
- Use only facts, not opinions.
- Use the past passive where necessary.
- Include key dates.

3 Plan a fact file about a famous place. Include information about each of the points in **2**.

4 Write your fact file. Include a picture of the place.

5 Display your fact files around the classroom. What interesting new facts did you learn?

eighty-five 85

PROJECT AND REVIEW

Make an audio tour guide about the past

Step 1

Research

> Decide how you are going to learn about the past.

- [ ] Work in pairs. Give examples of ways you can learn about the past in your local area.

Ways to learn about the past in our local area:

- You can visit the National Museum.
- You can do research in the local library.
- You can listen to a tour guide at … .

Step 2

Plan

> Find out about the history of an interesting place to visit.

- [ ] Write a list of questions to ask about the place you have chosen.
- [ ] Find the answers to the questions.
- [ ] Check the facts! Compare different sources.
- [ ] Collect photos of the place or of key events in its history.
- [ ] Plan the order of information in your audio guide.

Perge, Turkey

What?	An ancient Greek site with an amphitheater for 14,000 people.
What's it made of?	stone
Where?	Just outside Antalya, Turkey
When?	It dates back to 1300 BCE
Who?	Alexander the Great

86 eighty-six

Step 3

Create

✈ Write your script and record your audio guide.

- ☐ Write the script.
- ☐ What are you going to say in your introduction? Think of a way to make your listeners want to find out more.
- ☐ Include all the facts, using your Wh- questions.
- ☐ Decide who is going to read different sections of the audio guide.
- ☐ Are you going to use music or sound effects?
- ☐ Record your audio guide.

Meryam	Welcome to the ancient city of Perge! This city was built by the Greeks in 1300 BCE.
Berat	The building you can see in front of you used to be a school. Now, let's go and look at the old amphitheater.

➕ Find out about a historical place in your city. Visit with your family.

Step 4

Show and tell

✈ Present your audio guide.

- ☐ Play your audio guide to the class as they look at the photo(s) of the place you are describing.
- ☐ Discuss the audio guides. Which were most interesting or useful for tourists? Why?

Now I can …

- … use words to talk about the ancient Egyptians.
- … use the Past Passive to say how something was made.
- … ask questions using the Past Passive.
- … write a fact file.

eighty-seven 87

6 On the move!

How can I help exchange students in my town?

1 Look at the picture. Discuss.

What can you see?

What do you think?

What do you wonder?

I can see an airplane.

I think the children are excited.

I wonder where they are going.

Departures
Security →

2 You're going to catch a flight. Number the places in order.

CODE CRACKER

- check-in
- departure gate
- parking
- terminal
- security
- bus

3 Listen and write a sequence for Ahmed. Use the letters from the key.

- **P** = parking
- **C** = check in
- **B** = bus
- **S** = security
- **T** = terminal
- **DG** = departure gate

_____

Airports and travel
VOCABULARY

I will learn words for places in an airport.

1 🎧 047 Listen and look at the airport plan. Where are Esteban and Laura? Mark an ✗ on the map.

TERMINAL 2

Security | Check in | Baggage claim

DEPARTURES | | ARRIVALS

2 Listen again and complete the sentences.

> arrivals baggage check-in departure gate emigrating lands
> language exchange passport ~~security~~ takes off terminal

1 Laura and Esteban meet in line at __security__ in _____ 2.
2 Laura thought she saw Esteban in line at _____ .
3 Esteban is going to San Francisco on a _____ and Laura's family is _____ .
4 Laura has loads of _____ .
5 Their flight _____ at 11 o'clock and _____ at 5:30.
6 They have to go through _____ control and then go to their _____ .
7 Esteban's host family are meeting him in _____ .

3 🧩 Make a passport and cover for a partner. Ask and answer to complete the information.

90 ninety

4 Write the two reasons for moving or emigrating from **1**. Think of more reasons why people move to other countries. Discuss with a partner.

5 Read. Where are they? Match. There are two extra places.

1. Good morning, how many bags are you checking in today?
   Just these two, thank you.

2. Can I see your passport, please?

3. The plane is going to take off in 30 minutes. Please get ready to board.

4. Who are you meeting?
   My daughter – her plane landed 45 minutes ago so she'll be here soon.

6 Set up the classroom and role-play airports. Use your passports.

7 Create a map of an airport to help you remember the new words.

8 Listen to the chant. Stand up when you hear words with an *ire* sound and clap when you hear words with an *our/ower* sound.

We've been waiting for our flight for hours and hours.
The airport's a concrete jungle – no trees or flowers.
I think there's been a fire
Or the plane has burst a tire.
Can the air traffic controllers in their tower
Find us a plane and a pilot to hire?

9 Think of more words with the *ire* and *our/ower* sounds. Discuss with a partner.

ninety-one 91

Language lab

GRAMMAR 1: PRESENT PERFECT PROGRESSIVE

I will learn about the Present Perfect Progressive.

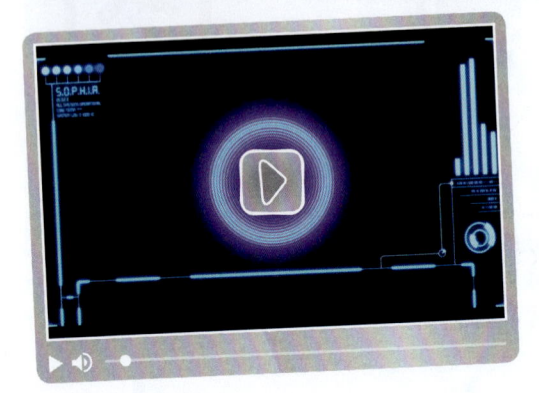

1 Watch the video.

I've **been waiting** in line at check-in for hours!
She's **been living** in Istanbul since 2016.
They **haven't been staying** with a host family.
Have you been studying English for long?

for = a duration of time
since = from a past date

2 Complete the sentences with **for** or **since**.

1. I've been studying Mandarin _____ five years.

2. We've been waiting for our flight to take off _____ ages!

3. He's been working as an airport security guard _____ last year.

4. A: Has it been raining _____ long here?
   B: No, it hasn't. Only _____ this morning.

3 🎧 💡 **Complete the questions. Then listen to Marco and write his answers.**

1 _____ (you/live) in São Paulo for long?
   _____

2 What _____ (you/do) since you arrived?
   _____

3 _____ (you/enjoy) school so far?
   _____

4 What _____ (you/learn) at school since you started?
   _____

5 _____ (you/study) Portuguese for long?
   _____

6 What _____ (your parents/do)?
   My mom _____ . My dad _____ .

4 💬 **Answer for you. Then ask and answer with a partner.**

1 How long have you been living in this city? _____
2 How long have you been studying English? _____
3 What have you been doing this week? _____
4 What have you been reading this week? _____

5 💡 **Read and answer.**

MATH ZONE

It's the year 2021 …

How long have you been living in London?

- I've been living here for five years. — **Mia**
- I've been living here since I was born. I'm 10 years old. — **William**
- I've been living here since 2017. — **Nijah**
- I've been living here since I was three. I'm 11 now. — **Javier**

1 Who's been living in London for the longest time? _____
2 Who's been living in London for the shortest time? _____
3 What's the total time the children have lived in London? _____

Story lab
READING

I will read a comic strip story.

1 💡 Read the first caption quickly. Where is the family moving to?

2 🎧 050 Read and listen. Check your answer to **1**.

LOST!

1
Hi, I'm Alex and this is my dad and my little sister, Amelie. We have been planning our family's move to Vietnam for what feels like ages! I can't believe we're finally here at the airport! We've just checked in all our big baggage (there was a lot!) and we're about to go through security.

Amelie, you've been eating that candy for ages. Please put it away. Now, where are the passports and boarding cards?

2
My mom has been working in Hanoi for six weeks and now we're going to live with her. We've been missing her a lot and it's been difficult for dad on his own – especially with a cheeky three-year-old!

Dad, where's Amelie?

Oh, no! I can't see her anywhere!

Don't worry, Dad – I'll ask a security guard.

3
We have to stick together – we don't want anyone else to get lost! We are walking towards the security guard when suddenly I spot something …

Look, Dad – it's a piece of Amelie's candy! And there's another one over there. I think if we follow it, we'll find her!

OK, but I'm going to tell the security guard about her first. Don't go anywhere without me, Alex!

4 We follow the candy trail out of departures, into an elevator, up to the second floor, past lots of cafés, and into arrivals. We can hear the security announcements asking people to look for Amelie. We are getting really anxious when suddenly …

Look, Dad! It's Amelie's teddy bear – we have been following the right trail!

Oh, thank goodness. Amelie! AMELIE!!!

5 We run across the arrivals area. And there's Amelie! She's been riding on someone else's baggage. Good job she didn't listen to Dad – she's been eating her candy all the time and that helped us find her!

Amelie – we were so worried.

I'm so sorry! I honestly didn't know she was there. I thought it was my son I've been pulling along. I forgot he was on my back!

6 We rush back to departures and board our plane. The rest of our journey goes really well and we finally start to relax, until we open Amelie's case …

Oh, dear!

Never mind – at least we have the right kid, Dad!

3 Read the story again and answer.

1 Who's been living in Hanoi for six weeks?
2 What do Dad and Alex follow to find Amelie?

Values Care for our world.

4 Think about the environment. What are the advantages and disadvantages of air travel? Discuss.

5 Tell the story from Dad's point of view. Then act it out in groups.

ninety-five 95

Experiment lab
TECHNOLOGY: IRIS RECOGNITION

I will learn about biometric technology.

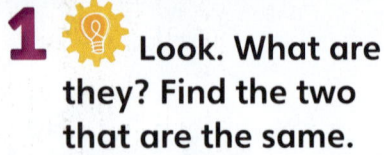

1 Look. What are they? Find the two that are the same.

Watch a video about iris recognition.

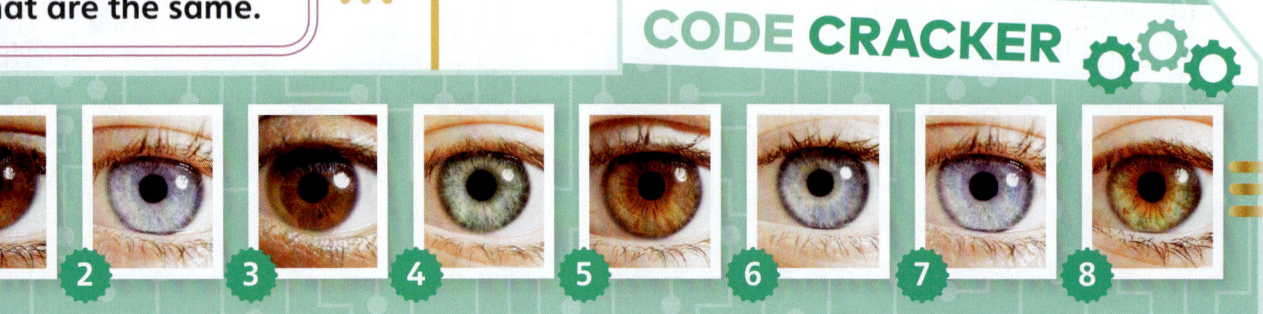

CODE CRACKER

1 2 3 4 5 6 7 8

2 Read and listen. What is biometrics?

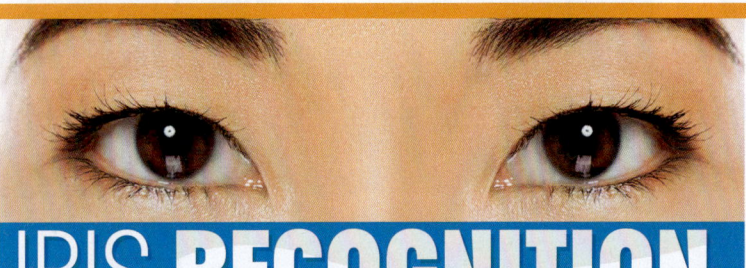

IRIS RECOGNITION

Our irises are the colored part of our eyes. Everyone's irises are different – even our own two irises are different! Scientists have been using biometrics, technology that looks at our bodies' unique features like irises and fingerprints, for many years. Biometrics uses mathematical pattern recognition. Have you seen science-fiction movies where doors open after scanning a person's eye? Well, that happens in the real world, too!

Airports have been using iris-recognition technology for a few years. Information about your iris is stored in a chip in your passport. Your iris then gets scanned. This means you don't have to see a person at passport control. The basic part of an iris scanner is just a digital camera. To use an iris scanner, you simply look into the camera. It takes images of your iris and matches them to the information in their database.

Passport control officers don't need to panic about their jobs yet, though! Until every airport in the whole world has iris-recognition technology, we'll still need people to check our passports.

3 Read again and circle T (True) or F (False).

1 Biometrics looks at our bodies' patterns. T / F
2 Biometrics is a very new technology. T / F
3 Our irises are the only unique feature of our body. T / F
4 The information from the iris scan is stored in your passport. T / F
5 Part of an iris scanner is a basic digital camera. T / F

4. Do you have any devices at home that use biometrics? Discuss.

- fingerprint recognition
- iris recognition
- voice recognition

"My mom's smartphone has fingerprint recognition."

"My tablet has voice recognition called "Siri"!"

5. Make funny glasses!

EXPERIMENT TIME

Can I recognize my classmates just from their eyes?

1. In pairs, take photos of each other's eyes.
2. Upload your eye images onto a computer. Create a database.
3. Print out your database.
4. Make predictions. How many eyes can you identify?
5. Check your predictions. Were they correct?

Important! DON'T use the flash when you take photos. It could damage your partner's eye!

	Prediction	Result
I'll recognize my own eye.		
I'll recognize my best friend's eye.		
How many eyes will I recognize in total?		

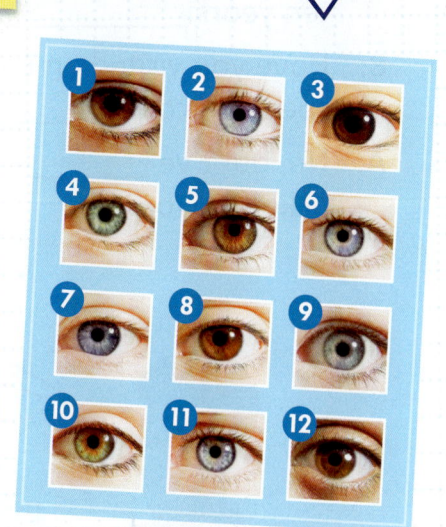

ninety-seven 97

Have we arrived yet?

COMMUNICATION: *JUST, ALREADY, YET, STILL*

I will talk about recent events.

Have you arrived at the airport **yet**?	Yes, we've **just** arrived here.
Have you checked in **already**?	Yes, I've **already** checked in online. But Marcos **still** hasn't checked in.

1 Read and complete with **just**, **already**, or **yet**.

1. **A:** I've _____ moved here so I haven't found work _____ .
   B: Don't worry – I've _____ seen this job board and I've _____ seen some jobs you might like.

2. **A:** I've been studying English for ten years _____ !
   B: Have you visited an English-speaking country _____ ?
   A: No, but I've _____ booked tickets to Toronto.

2 🎧 052 Listen to Martin and Alicia. Then circle T (True) or F (False).

1. Martin has just been at home. T / F
2. Alicia hasn't filled in the exchange form yet. T / F
3. Alicia has just started learning French. T / F
4. Martin hasn't taken his baggage off the bus yet. T / F
5. The bus is still there waiting. T / F

3 💬 💡 Play *Where are you?* Ask and answer with **just**, **already**, **yet**, and **still**.

1. parking
2. bus
3. terminal
4. check-in
5. security
6. cafés
7. departure gate
8. take off
9. landing
10. passport control
11. baggage claim
12. arrivals

Have you parked your car yet?

Have you gone through security yet?

Are you in a café?

Yes, I've already parked the car.

Yes, I've just gone through security.

Yes!

Writing lab
GIVING FEEDBACK

I will write a feedback form.

1 💡 **Look quickly at the text. Which emoji do you think the writer touched? Circle.**

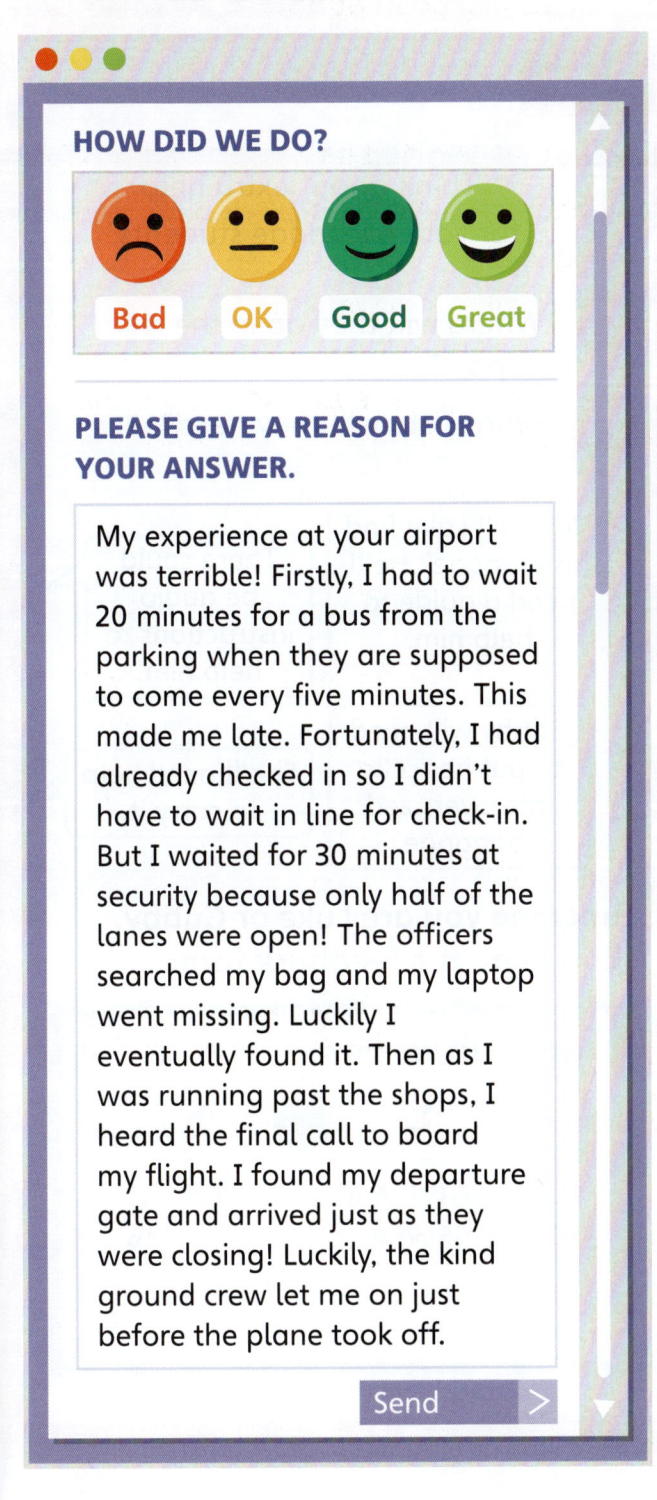

HOW DID WE DO?

😟 Bad   😐 OK   🙂 Good   😀 Great

PLEASE GIVE A REASON FOR YOUR ANSWER.

My experience at your airport was terrible! Firstly, I had to wait 20 minutes for a bus from the parking when they are supposed to come every five minutes. This made me late. Fortunately, I had already checked in so I didn't have to wait in line for check-in. But I waited for 30 minutes at security because only half of the lanes were open! The officers searched my bag and my laptop went missing. Luckily I eventually found it. Then as I was running past the shops, I heard the final call to board my flight. I found my departure gate and arrived just as they were closing! Luckily, the kind ground crew let me on just before the plane took off.

Send >

2 Read again. Circle.

1. Which things made the writer late?
   a. the bus from the parking
   b. waiting at check-in
   c. waiting at security
   d. losing his laptop
   e. waiting to board

2. How do you think the writer would review the ground crew?
   a. 😟 Bad   b. 😐 OK   c. 🙂 Good   d. 😀 Great

3 💬 **Work in pairs. Imagine a bad airport experience.**

What can go wrong in the following places?

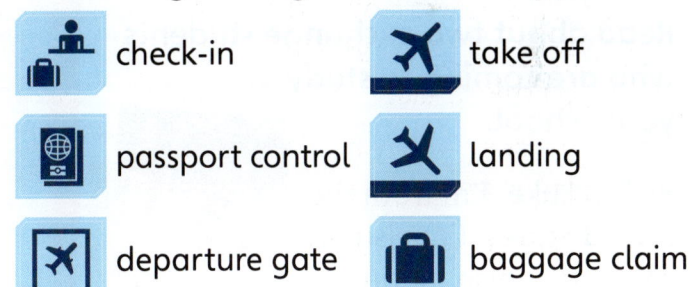

- check-in
- take off
- passport control
- landing
- departure gate
- baggage claim

4 ✳️ **Write your feedback forms.**

> Use adverbs to help describe a sequence of events and to add emphasis.

5 💡 **Read the feedback forms. Who imagined the worst airport experience?**

ninety-nine 99

PROJECT AND REVIEW

Create a welcome pack for exchange students to settle in your town

Step 1

Research

> Find out about your nearest airport.

- ☐ How many terminals are there?
- ☐ Which countries do the flights arrive from on a typical day?
- ☐ What special assistance is there for people with physical disabilities?
- ☐ Where does large personal baggage go?

Read about two exchange students who are coming to study at your school.

Hi, I'm Luke. I'm from the United States. I'm visually impaired which means I don't see very well. I use braille to read and have just started learning braille in your language, too!

Hi, I'm Gabby. I'm from the U.K. I've been looking forward to visiting your school for ages! I'm going to play the cello in your school orchestra. It's huge!

Step 2

Plan

> Think about extra help for your exchange students.

- ☐ Where will they go in the airport?
- ☐ What help will they need?

How will Luke find his luggage? He'll need a guide to help him.

There could be audio instructions to help him.

Gabby will need to put her cello into oversized baggage.

She'll need help to carry it.

Imagine you are Luke or Gabby. Complete the feedback form.

HOW DID WE DO?

😠 😐 🙂 😃

PLEASE GIVE A REASON FOR YOUR ANSWER.

Step 3

Create

> Create a multimedia welcome pack for your exchange students.

- ☐ Write an introduction about yourself and your experiences.
- ☐ Tell your exchange students what you have been learning in English class.
- ☐ Prepare other items for your welcome pack. Use the ideas below or think of your own.

I've been living here for seven years and I've been going to this school for three years. I'm also in the orchestra. I've been playing the French horn for five years …

- an audio guide to the airport
- a map of your school
- a video about yourself and your classmates
- top tips about your school

Step 4

Show and tell

> Practice using your welcome pack.

- ☐ Get into pairs. One of you is a Welcome Buddy and the other is one of the exchange students.
- ☐ Look through your welcome pack material together. Role-play.
- ☐ Swap roles.

So, you've been going to this school for six years? You will know all about it!

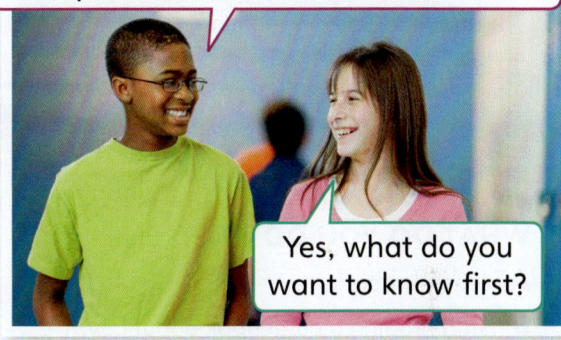

Yes, what do you want to know first?

Now I can …

- … use words to talk about airports and moving.
- … use the Present Perfect Progressive.
- … use *just*, *already*, *yet*, and *still*.
- … write a feedback form about a negative experience.

+ Research schools or organizations in your town that help newcomers. Find out what kind of information people new to your town need. Give them your ideas, too.

one hundred and one 101

3 Checkpoint
UNITS 5 AND 6

1 🎧 053 Listen and complete the quiz for Anya. Before you look at the results, guess what the results say about her. Then read and check.

Should you live in THE PAST, THE PRESENT, OR THE FUTURE?

1 WHICH ONE INTERESTS YOU MOST?
- A an archeology trip to find treasures
- B a language exchange to improve a language you are learning
- C a trip to Mars

2 DO YOU LIKE LEARNING ABOUT THE PAST?
- A Yes, history is my favorite class.
- B It's interesting most of the time.
- C Yes – but only when we use technology to make it interesting!

3 YOU'VE WON A TRIP TO CAIRO. WHAT DO YOU DO FIRST?
- A learn Arabic
- B start reading a guidebook about Egypt
- C exchange your ticket for a trip to a theme park

4 WHICH ONE IS TRUE FOR YOU?
- A I like traveling by train so that I can read while I am traveling.
- B I like getting to the airport early so that I am first in line at check-in.
- C I take very little baggage so that I can be first off the plane when it lands.

5 YOU HAVE DECIDED TO EMIGRATE. A MONTH LATER, YOU HAVE …
- A read about the country's history.
- B learned the language.
- C set up a videolink with your friends.

6 YOU HAVE JUST BEEN TO EGYPT ON VACATION. WHAT SOUVENIR DID YOU BRING HOME?
- A hieroglyphics on a piece of papyrus
- B a T-shirt
- C a selfie on Egypt's newest bridge

Now find out your results!

Mostly As You were born in the wrong century! You have a fantastic interest in the past. A knowledge of the past can help us – right now and also in the future.

Mostly Bs The present is the perfect place for you! You're enjoying your life right now. It's good to use your knowledge about the past to help you in the present, and to plan for the future.

Mostly Cs It's good to see how excited you are about the future! Keep learning about new technology – it's going to help the world in many different ways in the future.

CODE CRACKER

2 Can you figure out the word on Anya's piece of papyrus? Then write your own word in hieroglyphics. Give it to a partner to figure out!

___ ___ ___ ___

3 Read the fact file from Anya's guidebook and answer the questions.

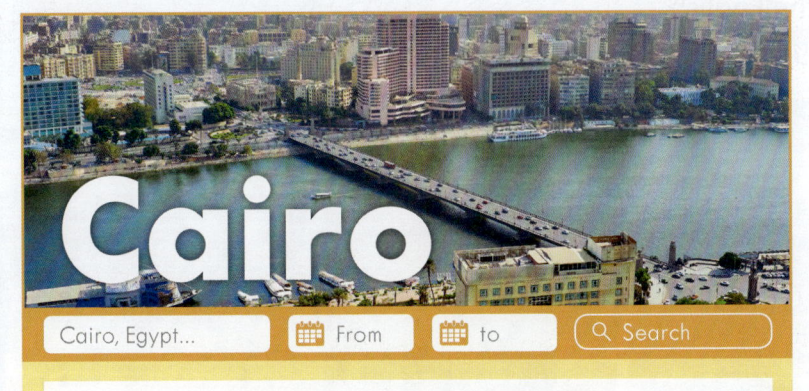

Cairo

Cairo, Egypt... | From | to | Search

- Cairo's history dates back to 969 CE.
- The River Nile runs through Cairo, and there are two islands in the middle of the city.
- It is a very crowded city. About 22 million people live in or near Cairo and there are about 4.5 million cars.
- The oldest museum in Cairo, the Egyptian Museum, opened in 1835 with more than 160,000 of Egypt's most valuable treasures. But it was too small and in 2020 the museum moved to a big, new, modern building.

1 How old is the city?
_____

2 What is interesting about the river?
_____

3 How many people live in or near Cairo?
_____

4 When was the oldest museum in Cairo built?
_____

5 How many artifacts did the museum have when it opened?
_____

6 When did it move to a new building, and why?
_____

4 Use the information in the fact file to write an email from Anya to a friend.

- What has Anya learned about Cairo, including its history, culture, etc.?
- What interesting building has she visited?
- What does she find interesting about the country?

5 Look back at the quiz. Ask and answer with a partner. Find out how many of your classmates have the same results as you.

one hundred and three 103

The United Kingdom
CULTURE

The United Kingdom

The United Kingdom (U.K.) is made up of the countries of England, Scotland, Wales, and Northern Ireland. The capital of the U.K. is London, in England. The U.K. is famous for soccer, pop and rock bands, its traditional castles, and, of course, the English language. The U.K. has been invaded many times in its history and because of this the English language is a mixture of a lot of different languages.

Fun Fact!

The British drink over 163 million cups of tea daily, about 20 times the number consumed by Americans.

1 Read and listen. Which famous stone is mentioned in the text?

THE BRITISH MUSEUM

London is famous for its many museums and art galleries. For fans of ancient history and civilizations, the best London museum to visit is the British Museum.

The British Museum has the largest collection of ancient Egyptian treasures outside Egypt. There are an estimated 14 million pieces in the collection, but the museum only displays about four percent of this. The collection on permanent display contains mummies, coffins, wall paintings from inside tombs, and sculptures of pharaohs.

One of the most famous ancient Egyptian objects in the British Museum is the Rosetta Stone. The Rosetta Stone was the key to understanding hieroglyphics. In the past, archeologists knew that hieroglyphics could tell them a lot about ancient Egyptians. But they couldn't read them!

The stone was found in 1799. It had the same thing written on it in three different languages, including hieroglyphics and ancient Greek. Because scholars understood Greek they could try and translate the hieroglyphics. The problem was that the stone was broken. It took a long time to try and match the pieces together so that they made sense. Eventually though, scholars began to understand hieroglyphics and they realized how smart the ancient Egyptians were.

The Rosetta Stone is one of the most visited items in the British Museum. However, the Egyptians wanted to have it back. In 2005, the British Museum presented Egypt with an exact copy which is displayed at the Rashid National Museum in northern Egypt, very close to where the stone was found.

2 Read again and answer.

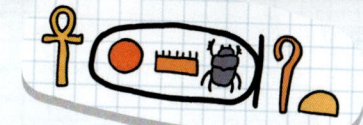

1 How many treasures does the Egyptian collection have in total?
_____

2 What did the Rosetta Stone help people to understand?
_____

3 Where is the copy of the Rosetta Stone?
_____

3 Design your own Rosetta Stone inscription.

4 Listen. In which U.K. city are Cameron and Mihai?

5 Listen again. Circle.

1 Which part of the airport didn't Cameron mention?
   a security
   b passport control
   c baggage claim

2 At which London landmark do Cameron and Mihai meet?
   a Buckingham Palace
   b Big Ben
   c Trafalgar Square

3 What's the London Underground?
   a an airport
   b a train system
   c a museum

4 Which museum don't they decide to visit?
   a Science Museum
   b London Transport Museum
   c The National Gallery

5 Which U.K. city are they going to next?
   a Cardiff
   b Edinburgh
   c Belfast

My Culture

6 Read and discuss.

1 What famous museums are there in your city/country?
2 What's the best museum you've visited? Why?
3 Why are museums important?

A famous museum in my city is the Frida Kahlo Museum.

one hundred and five 105

7 I hate it when ...

How can I design a board game about fears?

1 Look and discuss. How does the photo make you feel?

- No way! I don't ever want to do that!
- It looks fun. I'm not scared!
- I've done that!

2 Look at the list. How do you feel about these things?

Ten things many people feel NERVOUS about

1. heights
2. spiders and snakes
3. slipping on something and falling over
4. getting lost
5. falling asleep in class
6. flying
7. turning off the internet
8. going to the dentist
9. bees
10. speaking a foreign language

3 Work in groups. Choose three things you all agree you want to avoid.

4 Add more ideas to the list. Compare with other groups.

Oh, no!
VOCABULARY

I will learn words to describe challenging situations.

1 Complete the questions with the missing words.

> a banana skin   called   dropped   got lost   overslept   skyscraper
> slept alone   the internet   the wrong person   your words

HAVE YOU EVER ...?

1 _____ and missed the start of class

forgotten 2 _____ on stage

slipped on 3 _____

4 _____ your phone

texted 5 _____

6 _____ in a maze

7 _____ your teacher "Mom" by mistake

turned off 8 _____

looked down from the top of a 9 _____

10 _____ in the dark

2 Work in pairs. Use the situations in **1** or your own ideas. Ask your partner. How many *Yes* answers does your partner have?

> Have you ever overslept and missed the start of class?

> No, I haven't! My turn.

> Have you ever forgotten the date of a friend's birthday?

> Er ... yes, I have. I've forgotten when yours is!

3 Work in pairs. Think and discuss.

1. What's the scariest experience you've ever had?
2. What's the most embarrassing experience you've ever had?

4 Listen. Circle the letter sounds we don't hear when we say these words.

> Wrap this bandage around your wrist.

> I hurt my thumb when I was climbing a tree.

5 Listen to the words again and repeat.

> I don't know how to tie a knot!

> The moon is bright on a dark night.

6 Listen. Circle the silent letter sounds.

1. Be careful with that knife. I'm frightened of blood.
2. I've written a message to the wrong person – my neighbor just answered, not my friend!
3. I don't like climbing trees. I'm scared of heights.
4. I wrote an exam and answered every question wrong!

one hundred and nine 109

Language lab

GRAMMAR 1: PRESENT PERFECT AND SIMPLE PAST

I will learn about the Present Perfect and Simple Past.

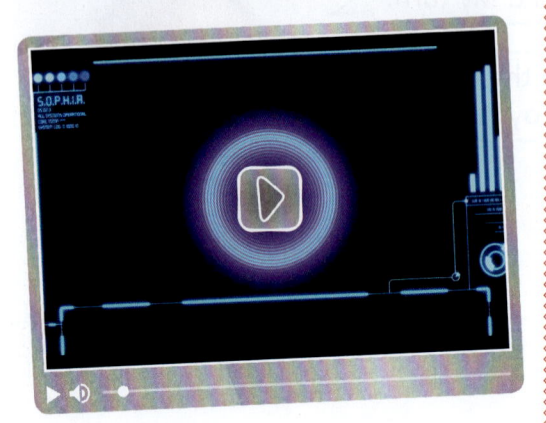

1 Watch the video.

Present Perfect
Have you ever **taken** a ride in a helicopter?

Yes, I **have**.

Simple Past
When did you do that?

I **went** in a helicopter last summer/two weeks ago/when I was eight/in July!

2 Write questions and complete the answers. Use the Present Perfect or Simple Past.

1 A: you ever/see/a shark?
   _____
   B: Yes, I _____ !

2 A: When/you/see it?
   _____
   B: I/see/one in the ocean, last summer.
   _____

3 A: your parents/take you for a ride/ on a Ferris wheel?
   _____
   B: Yes, they _____ .

4 A: When/you/go?
   _____
   B: We/go/there two weeks ago.
   _____

5 A: you ever/forget/a school book?
   _____
   B: Yes, I/leave/my math book at home yesterday.
   _____

6 A: you ever/swim/in a river?
   _____
   B: No, I _____ , but last weekend, I/swim/in the sea.
   _____

110 one hundred and ten

3 Listen and complete.

Find someone who has ...	Name	When did it happen?
1 forgotten to bring things to school.	Veronika	
2 slipped on ice.	Diego	
3 lost something important.	Mario	
4 climbed a tree and got stuck.		at the age of five
5 turned off the internet for more than two days.	Diego	
6 fallen asleep in class.		yesterday

4 Work in groups. Write two more questions. Then play *Find someone who ...* .

5 Can you find your way out of the maze? Give your partner instructions to follow.

CODE CRACKER

Go straight. Then turn left.

I've turned left, but I can't go forward now ...

No, you've turned too soon.

6 Make a chatterbox. Write questions in the Present Perfect and Simple Past.

one hundred and eleven 111

Story lab
READING

I will read a conversation.

1 💡 **Work in pairs. Look at the text and the pictures. Discuss.**

1. What is the story about?
2. Who are the characters? Where are they? What are they doing?

2 🎧 **Read and listen. Check your answers.**

The challenge

Luis and Josie are doing a Nature challenge. Let's see how well they did!

NATURE CHALLENGE

Don't forget to show us the things you have done.

Have you …?

- found a bird's feather ✓
- written your name in nature ☐
- picked up a smooth stone ☐
- seen a snake ☐
- crossed the river ☐
- walked through a rock tunnel ☐

1 Luis, where are you? All the other kids have gone into the tunnel already. We're last! Have you crossed the river yet?

Yes, I have. I jumped across some rocks in the river. Sorry, Josie. I know it's taken me a long time. I fell off one of the stepping stones so I've been sitting on the grass next to the river, waiting for my shoes to dry. But I've picked up a beautiful smooth stone! See you soon.

2 Luis????? I'm still waiting. What's happened to you?

Sorry – I got lost! I took the wrong path through the forest. Then I saw a nest up high in a tree so I climbed up to have a look.

Oh, great. Did you take a photo of the nest?

No, I dropped my phone. Luckily it fell into the soft grass so it isn't broken.

Oh, Luis!

3 Read the Nature challenge and check ✓ the things Luis and Josie have done.

Josie is getting more and more angry. Luis still hasn't appeared! She calls him again. She is not pleased with his progress.

3 Have you written your name somewhere?

Yes, I went to the beach and wrote it on the sand. But I haven't got a photo of it because just after I wrote it, a wave came and washed it away!

4 Hey, I've just found a beautiful peacock feather. And you've got a smooth stone, so that's two things.

Sorry, Josie. I've just put my hand in my pocket and the stone isn't there. There's a hole in my pocket and it's fallen out. I've lost it.

LUIS!!! I'm going to scream!

Luis hears Josie scream. He thinks she's screaming because she's angry with him ...

5 *Aaaagh! LUIS!!!*

I'll be there soon. We'll finish the challenge in time, don't worry.

That's not the problem. I've just seen a snake!

6 Did you take a photo of it?

No, of course not! I ran away as fast as I could! But I have just seen something else ...

Values Challenge yourself.

4 Add three more challenges to the list. Act out the story with a partner.

5 Think and discuss.
1 Why is it important to set ourselves challenges?
2 What can we do when things go wrong?

one hundred and thirteen 113

Experiment lab
SCIENCE: WHAT HAPPENS WHEN WE FEEL FEAR?

I will learn about fear.

1 Think and discuss. Have you ever been afraid? How did it feel?

Watch a video about fear.

2 Complete the text with the words.

> beat breathe eat freeze
> reduce see stand think

Feel the fear

When we experience fear, our body prepares for "fight or flight". This means we have to make the decision to face the thing we are afraid of or to run away from it. Humans have always reacted to fear in this way.

Brain
When you are afraid, your brain can't **1** _____ about anything else except what to do about the scary situation. Your brain tells your body to get ready for fight or flight.

Heart and lungs
You **2** _____ faster and more oxygen enters your blood. Your heart starts to **3** _____ faster so that the blood flows to your muscles.

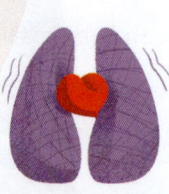

Eyes
The pupils in your eyes grow bigger so that you can **4** _____ more clearly.

Digestive system
Your digestive system slows down so that the body can focus on dealing with the fear. That is why it is so difficult to **5** _____ anything when you feel scared.

Body temperature
We sweat when we are afraid. This is the body's way of trying to **6** _____ its temperature.

Hair
Have you ever looked at a cat's hair when it is afraid? The same thing used to happen to people long ago when they had more body hair than we have today. Their skin became tight and this made the hairs on their arms and necks **7** _____ straight up.

Muscles
Sometimes we feel our knees become weak. This also happens in the animal world. Have you ever seen a rabbit **8** "_____" in front of a car's lights at night? This is the body's way of trying to appear "invisible" so that it will escape danger.

3 Work in pairs. Figure out how fast your heart beats!

MATH ZONE

1. Place the first two fingers (not the thumb) of your left hand on your neck or on the inside of your wrist.
2. When you have found your heartbeat, count how many beats you feel in 30 seconds (use a watch or clock with a second hand).
3. Multiply this number by two and that will tell you how many times your heart beats per minute.

4 Work in groups. Think and discuss.

What can you do to help yourself when you feel scared?

I always breathe in slowly, count to ten, then breathe out. It relaxes me.

EXPERIMENT TIME

Measuring heart rate

1. Look at the experiment. When will your heart beat the fastest/slowest? Write your predictions.
2. Do the experiment. Make sure you rest for two minutes after each activity for your heartbeat to return to normal.
3. Write your results. What do you learn from the results about exercise and how fast your heart beats?

Physical activity	My prediction (Will my heart beat faster or slower?)	Results (beats per minute)
1 Run on the spot for one minute.		
2 Stand, relaxed, for one minute.		
3 Walk around the room for three minutes.		
4 Run on the spot for three minutes.		
5 Do 20 jumping jacks.		

one hundred and fifteen

I'm going to talk about ... !

COMMUNICATION: GIVING A PRESENTATION

I will learn about giving a presentation.

1 Listen to the conversation and answer the questions.
1. Why is Isabel nervous?
2. What happened when Isabel last gave a presentation?

2 Read the tips. Are the presenters following the advice? Check ✓ or cross ✗.

1
2
3
4

TIPS

- Plan your presentation.
  - Introduce the topic. I'm going to talk about ...
  - Use personal experiences. Have you ever ...? I remember .../It happened to me when ...
  - Order your points. Firstly,/Secondly,/Then/Finally, ...
  - End the presentation. In conclusion .../To summarize ...
- Write key points on cards.
- Use short, simple sentences.
- Speak clearly and loudly.
- Practice your presentation. Record yourself and listen.
- Make eye contact!

3 Number these sentences from a presentation in order.

- a First of all, they are an essential part of our ecosystem and the food chain!
- b I used to do the same, but then I thought more carefully about spiders.
- 1 c Today I'm going to talk about spiders!
- d In conclusion, spiders are part of our natural world and we should respect them as we respect all living things.
- e Secondly, we should remember that most spiders are not dangerous at all.
- f How many of you have run away from a tiny spider?

4 Complete the question and write a short presentation about it. Then present it to the class.

Why are we afraid of ...?

Writing lab
WRITING A DIALOG

I will write a dialog.

1 **Complete the dialog with the missing sentences. Listen and check.**

A man is walking past a house when he sees a sign outside: "For sale: My talking dog". The man knocks on the door.

Man: Hello! Are you the owner of the talking dog?
Owner: (*proudly*) Yes, I am! Come in. (*They walk into the living room.*) This is my dog, Claude!
Dog: (*woof woof*)
Man: (*nervously*) Hello, Claude. I've never met a talking dog before. **1** ____ Have you had a lot of adventures?
Dog: (*politely*) Yes, I've lived all over the world, even in the Alps.
Man: (*with interest*) Really? **2** ____
Dog: About five years ago. I had a job there. **3** ____
Man: Wow! That sounds scary.
Dog: I wasn't scared! I've also climbed Mount Kilimanjaro and swum across Lake Victoria. **4** ____
Man: (*looking at the dog's owner, surprised*) What an amazing dog! **5** ____
Owner: (*angrily*) Because none of it is true! **6** ____

a. When did you do that?
b. And now I read to children at school.
c. I had to rescue people from avalanches.
d. He hasn't done any of those things!
e. Tell me what you've done with your life.
f. Why do you want to sell him?

2 Find and underline an example of the following in the dialog.
1. a character's actions
2. where the action happens (location)
3. the way a character speaks
4. sounds
5. the punctuation used to introduce a character's words

3 Write a dialog.

4 Work in pairs or small groups. Choose people to play each character. Practice reading your dialogs aloud.

one hundred and seventeen 117

PROJECT AND REVIEW

Design and make a board game about fears

Step 1

Research

> Compare the features of board games.

- [ ] Brainstorm all the board games you know.
- [ ] Make a list of the features of each game.
  - How many players play?
  - What do you need in order to play? dice, counters, cards …
- [ ] Make a list of the features you would like to have in your board game.

FEATURES
It's a game for more than two players.
It's a race to finish.
It's easy to play.
It's for all ages.

YOU NEED:
Dice
Counters (a coin, an eraser, etc.)
Cards describing situations

Step 2

Plan

> Design your board game.

- [ ] Plan the route from start to finish. How will players move along the route?
- [ ] Write a list of challenges where players have to talk about real situations and decide what they would do.
- [ ] Write a list of positive situations and situations where something has gone wrong. What should the player do for each?
- [ ] Think of a name for your game.

Talk about the last time you felt scared.

If you had to eat an insect, would you be scared?

You have lost your way. Go back two spaces.

You have found some treasure! Go forward three spaces.

One of your team members has slipped on ice. You have to take them to the hospital. Miss a turn.

Step 3

Create

> ✈ Make your board game.

- ☐ Write a short description of the game.
- ☐ Write the rules. Make sure they are simple and easy to follow.
- ☐ On cards, write sentences to describe positive, negative, and challenging situations.
- ☐ Make the board and character pieces for your game.

SCARY SITUATION

You and your friend are in a plane ready to sky dive. You look out the window. It's so high up! You feel your heart beating fast. Your hands are sweaty. What do you do?

➕ Ask your family about their fears. Are they the same as yours?

Step 4

Show and tell

> ✈ Play your board game.

- ☐ Give your game to another group to play.
- ☐ Read the rules and play the game.
- ☐ Discuss the games. What did people like about your game? What didn't they like?
- ☐ What could you do differently or better?

Now I can ...

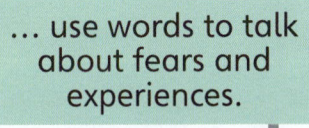

- ... use words to talk about fears and experiences.
- ... use the Present Perfect and the Simple Past to talk about experiences.
- ... give a presentation.
- ... write a dialog.

one hundred and nineteen

8 My amazing city

How can I create a project to change my city?

1 Look and discuss. What can you see?

2 💡 **Look at the picture. What do you expect to see in this city?**

modern skyscrapers

traditional buildings

stadiums

parks

tunnels

bridges

3 💡 **Find north. Then play.**

I'm facing south-east.

Correct!

one hundred and twenty-one 121

Downtown
VOCABULARY

I will learn words for buildings and structures in towns and cities.

1 Read the text quickly and answer the questions. Then listen and read.

1 Which buildings are modern?
2 Which buildings are old?

NEW TOWN

Welcome to New Town – the perfect place to live, work, and study! We have a mixture of modern buildings like **skyscrapers**, **office buildings** and our new sports **stadium**, and old buildings like the old **city hall** in the town square, with its beautiful nineteenth-century **statue**. New Town is a student town with a **university** near the river, but also a working town with office buildings and a **factory**.

New Town is a safe city to walk around with wide **sidewalks**, cycle lanes, and plenty of **crosswalks**. Most of the traffic is taken away from the downtown area by an **overpass** or a **tunnel**.

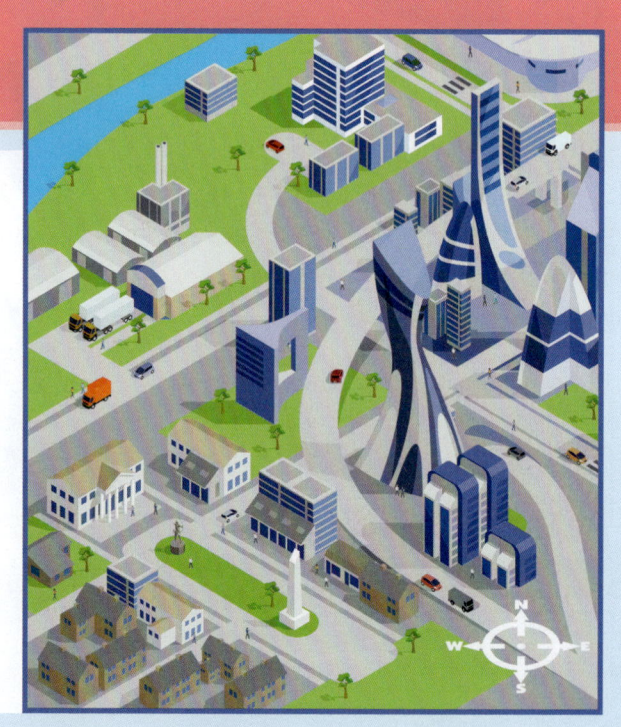

We hope you enjoy your visit!

2 Match the words to make compound nouns.

1 sky   2 cross   3 over   4 side   5 city   6 office

a walk   b hall   c building   d scraper   e walk   f pass

3 Use the words from **2** to label the photos. Check ✓ the things in your city.

1 2 3 4 5 6

_____ _____ _____ _____ _____ _____

4 Write the place next to the correct definition.

factory   stadium   statue   tunnel   university

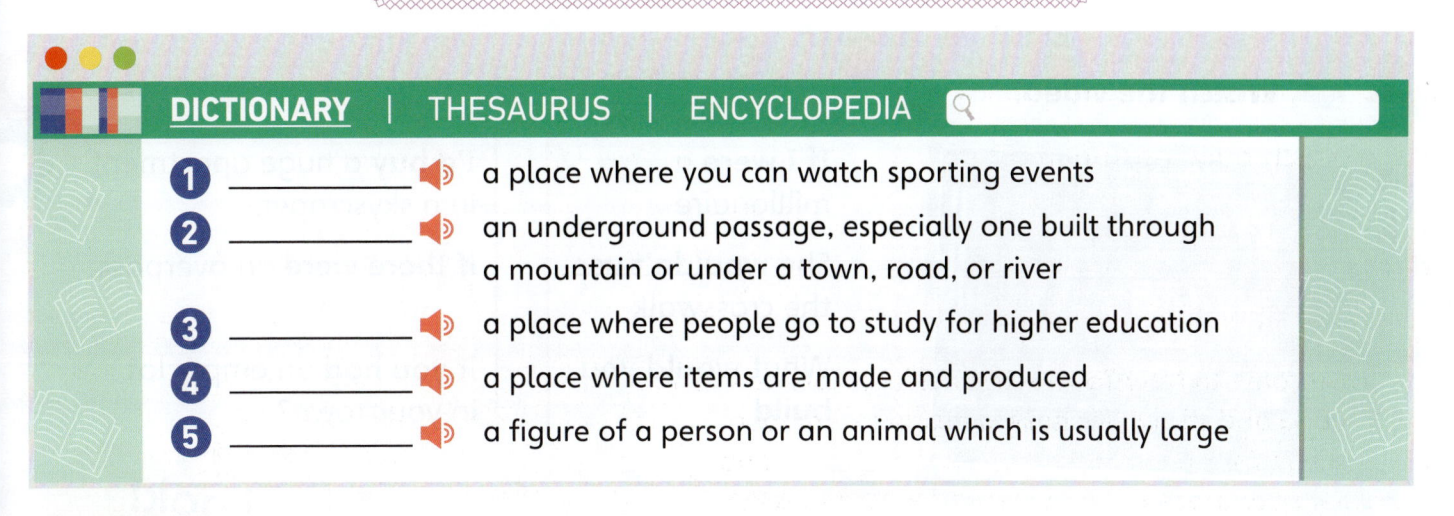

DICTIONARY | THESAURUS | ENCYCLOPEDIA

1. _____ a place where you can watch sporting events
2. _____ an underground passage, especially one built through a mountain or under a town, road, or river
3. _____ a place where people go to study for higher education
4. _____ a place where items are made and produced
5. _____ a figure of a person or an animal which is usually large

5 Make a small statue of yourself.

Use clay to make your statue.

Display your statues.

6 Create a city map to help you remember the new words.

7 Listen and sort. Then say the words.

elegant city   European city
hospital   hour   office building
one-way street   underground train
university

a	an
_____	_____
_____	_____
_____	_____
_____	_____

8 Add more words that start with a vowel to the *a* group.

Language lab

GRAMMAR 1: SECOND CONDITIONAL

I will learn the second conditional.

1 Watch the video.

If I were a millionaire	,	I'd buy a huge apartment in a skyscraper.
She wouldn't use the crosswalk		if there were an overpass.
What would you build		if you had an empty lot in your town?

Look!
can → could
must → had to

2 Complete the second conditional sentences.

1 If I _____ (be) you, I _____ (move) to a bigger city.
2 If you _____ (not drive), _____ (walk) more?
3 The city _____ (be) really congested with cars if there _____ (not be) an overpass.
4 If my parents _____ (have) more money, they _____ (buy) a bigger apartment.
5 I _____ (not like) it if my school _____ (be) at the top of a skyscraper!
6 She _____ (live) in Miami if she _____ (can).

124 one hundred and twenty-four

3 Listen and check ✓.

1 What would the girl do to her city if they had more money?

a ☐   b ☐   c ☐

2 Which idea won the environmental competition?

a ☐   b ☐   c ☐

4 Look at the entries to the environmental competition in 3. Then discuss.

1 How would each entry help the environment?
2 What environmental project would you do in your city if you could?

> Putting solar panels on the roof of the city hall would produce renewable energy.

> If I did an environmental project, I'd create …

5 Complete the sentences with your ideas from 4.

1 If we created cycle lanes in the city, _____ .
2 If there were fewer cars in the city, _____ .
3 If you put solar panels on the city hall, _____ .

6 Play Chain Game.

CODE CRACKER

> If I won a lot of money, I'd buy a horse.

> If I bought a horse, …

one hundred and twenty-five 125

Story lab
READING

I will read a poem.

1 Look at the story. What's special about it?

2 Read and listen. Check your answer to **1**.

THE LIFE
SWAP

If I could, I'd move to the city.
I love the country; it's green and pretty,
But the long dark nights
Don't compare to the exciting bright lights.
One day I'll move to the city.

If I could, I'd move to a small country town.
The cars and the noise are getting me down.
I dream of birds and of bees,
Of flowers and trees,
One day I'll move to the country.

If I could find another dreamer like me,
We would swap places for a week or three.
We could put both places to the test
And find which we like the best.
I've found another dreamer like me.

I've been in the city a day and a night
And it doesn't quite feel right.
Busy sidewalks and crossways,
Constant traffic every day,
If I knew that, I wouldn't have come.

Country life is a surprise and a shock!
I never thought I'd miss the city blocks.
But there are forests and a lake,
And friends are easy to make.
I'll stay a bit longer, I think.

Now more time has passed.
I'm happy in the city at last.
If I ever miss my country town,
I go to the park downtown
And lie in the sun on the grass.

I love my new country life!
It's a perfect place to raise kids with my wife.
If I ever miss the city,
We take a train ride so pretty
And visit our family and friends.

3 Read the poem again. Then read the diary entries. Draw arrows → to show where each of these events happen in the poem.

CODE CRACKER

1 Saturday 17th

It's my wedding day today! I never thought that when I left the city a year and a half ago I'd be marrying a country girl and buying a house together! I met my future wife during my first weeks in the country when I was walking by the lake. She loves visiting my friends and family in the city, but we have decided to raise a family here in the country. Better go – I don't want to be late for my wedding!

2 Thursday 3rd

Today I met the girl I connected with on the city/country exchange site. We've been messaging for a few weeks now. She wants to exchange her house in a small country town for my apartment in the city. Let's see what happens …!

3 Tuesday 29th

I'm leaving the country and moving to the city today. I'm nervous, but I'm excited. If I changed my mind, I would be able to go back and live with my parents, but I'm sure I won't. I've been dreaming of this moment for a long time!

Values Choose your environment.

4 Imagine what happened to the man or the woman in their first weeks in their new homes. Compare your ideas.

5 Think and discuss.

1. What are the advantages and disadvantages of living in a city?
2. What are the advantages and disadvantages of living in the country?
3. Where would you prefer to live?

Experiment lab
DESIGN: WATER FEATURES

I will learn about the design of water features.

1 Look at the water features. Which do you like best? Discuss with a partner.

Watch a video about water fountains.

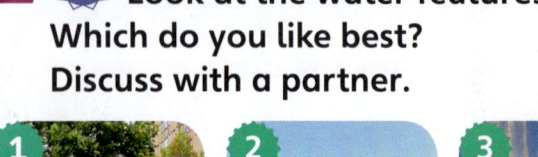

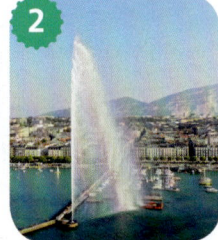

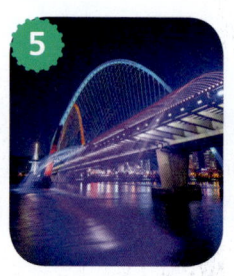

1 2 3 4 5 6

2 Read and listen. What does the article say we like to throw into water?

CREATIVE WATER FEATURES IN CITIES

Designers are doing lots of creative things with water. Plazas and parks provide water in all sorts of forms: waterfalls, water walls, water jets, tranquil pools, water tunnels, and fountains of all kinds.

Why do we like to see water in a city? Water makes a change from the straight lines and gray color of a city environment. People like to see the natural world around them. You'll also see a big change in people's behavior around water features. One of the best things about water is the feel of it. People love to touch it. Water makes us want to stop and look at it, touch it, throw stones or coins in it. We like to put our hands in it, dip our toes and feet in it, and sometimes even splash about in it. Nowadays, the design of many water features actively encourages children to get in and play. And if you thought that all these water features would mean a lot of wasted water, don't worry! The water is reused and continuously pumped around.

water jets

fountain

water wall

3 Read again and answer.

1 What six types of water feature are mentioned in the article?
_____ _____ _____ _____ _____ _____

2 Why do we like to see water features in cities?
_____

3 Which of these things is not mentioned in the article? Circle.

a   b   c   d

4 Figure it out! Compare with a partner.

MATH ZONE

The fountain in my town pumps 5 liters of water every second. How much water does it pump in a minute? In an hour?

5 Use your water pump to design a water feature.

Materials
- a plastic bottle
- a straw
- a balloon
- a plastic bowl (big enough to hold all the water from the bottle)

EXPERIMENT TIME

Create a water pump!

1 Make a small hole midway up the plastic bottle.
2 Put a straw in the hole. Push through so it touches the bottom of the bottle.
3 Put super glue around the hole to seal it. Wait for it to dry.
4 Fill the bottle with water. Place the bowl under the straw.
5 Predict what will happen when you put a blown-up balloon on the top of the bottle. Try it out!

Can you think of any pumps you use at home?

one hundred and twenty-nine 129

Go over the bridge, …
COMMUNICATION: PREPOSITIONS OF MOVEMENT

I will ask for and give directions.

across   along   past   over   around   through

1 🎧 068 **Read and complete with the prepositions of movement. Then listen and check.**

Woman: Hi there! I've been walking **1** _____ for ages and I can't find the stadium. Please can you tell me where it is?

Man: Sure! I'd go **2** _____ the park – it's the quickest way.

Woman: How do I get to the park?

Man: Go **3** _____ this street and **4** _____ the gate over there. Walk **5** _____ the park and through the gate on the opposite side. Go **6** _____ the overpass and you'll see a big statue in front of you. Go **7** _____ the statue, **8** _____ an office building, and you'll see the stadium.

Woman: Uh thank you. Can you write that down for me?

Look!
Please can you tell me where the stadium is?
How do I get to the stadium?

2 🎧 069 💡 **Listen and follow. Where do Marco and Miriam want to go?**

3 💬 **Think about your school. Give each other directions.**

Excuse me, can you tell me where the gym is?

Sure! Go out of this classroom, turn left, go along the hallway, through the doors … .

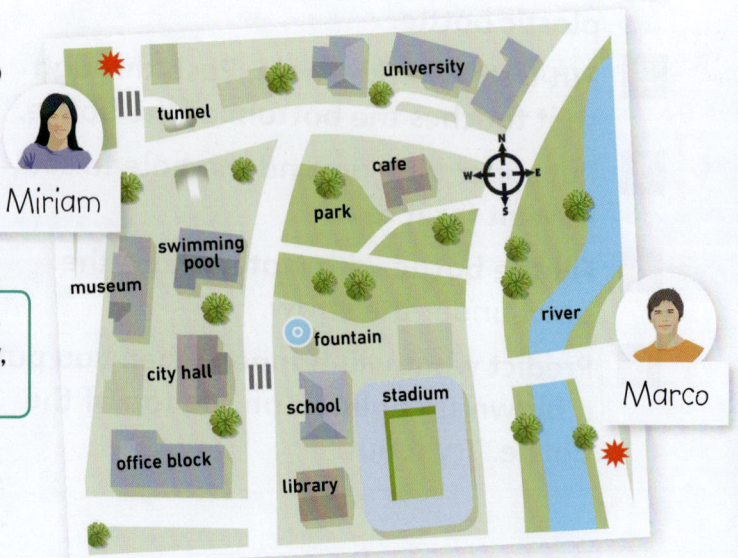

Writing lab
WRITING INSTRUCTIONS

I will write instructions in an email.

1 Look quickly at the email. Where are they going to meet?

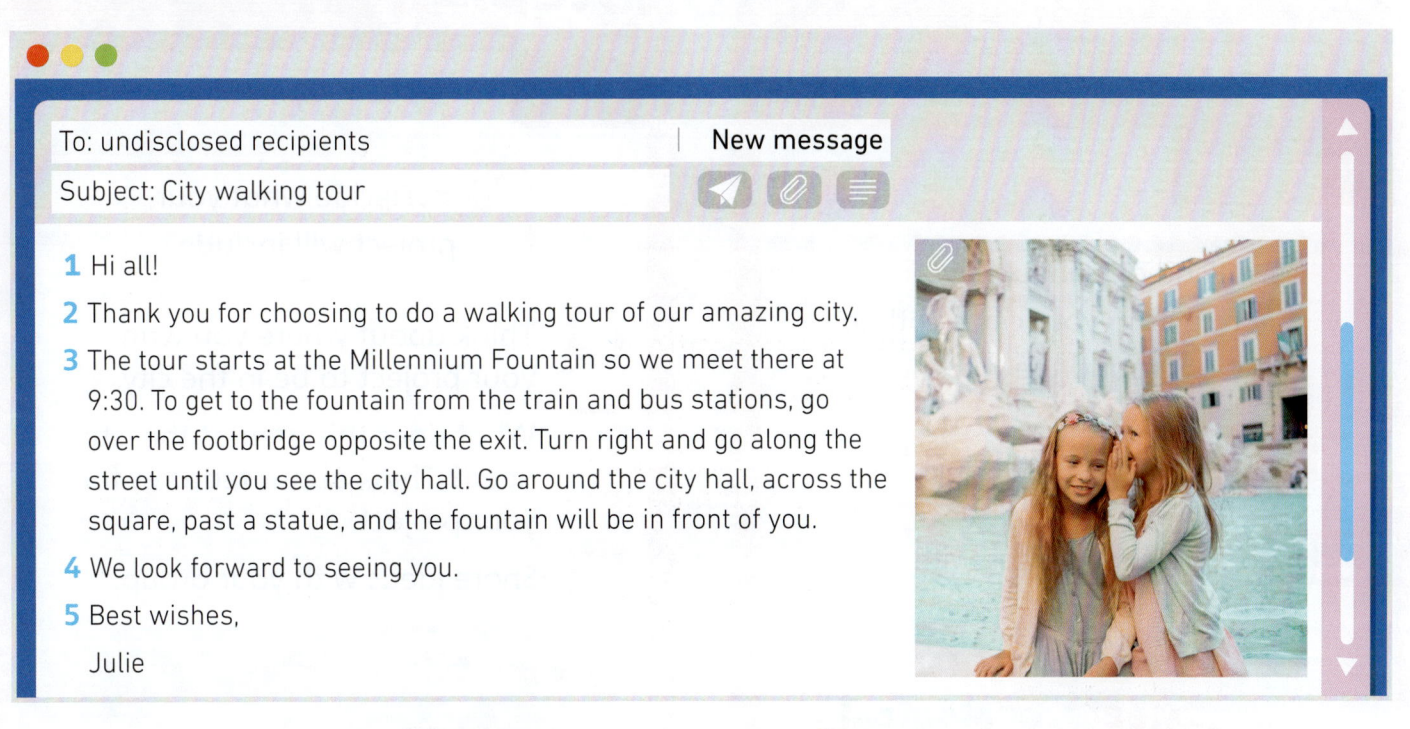

To: undisclosed recipients | New message
Subject: City walking tour

1 Hi all!

2 Thank you for choosing to do a walking tour of our amazing city.

3 The tour starts at the Millennium Fountain so we meet there at 9:30. To get to the fountain from the train and bus stations, go over the footbridge opposite the exit. Turn right and go along the street until you see the city hall. Go around the city hall, across the square, past a statue, and the fountain will be in front of you.

4 We look forward to seeing you.

5 Best wishes,
 Julie

---

2 Read again. Write the paragraph number from the email.

body of email ____   greeting ____
closing ____   sign off ____
introduction ____

3 💡 Look and sort.

Dear   Hello   Kind regards
Sincerely   Yours truly

Greetings	Sign offs

4 💡 Plan the instructions for the body of your email. Then write your email.

A group of people are visiting your city. Where will they arrive? Where will you meet? Note down directions.

_____
_____
_____

Use the imperative form for instructions.

5 🌀 Draw a map to attach to your email.

PROJECT AND REVIEW

Create a project to change your city

Step 1

Research

> Find out about city projects in your city or other cities around the world.

☐ Find the best city project for each of these words.

☐ Compare your ideas with a partner.

best water feature
innovative   **ecological**
modern

> I think Supertree Grove in Singapore is the best ecological project.

> I think it's an innovative project, too.

Step 2

Plan

> Decide what your project will include.

☐ Think about where you want your project to be in the city.

☐ What does this area of the city need? Think about features for your project.

☐ Share ideas with your group.

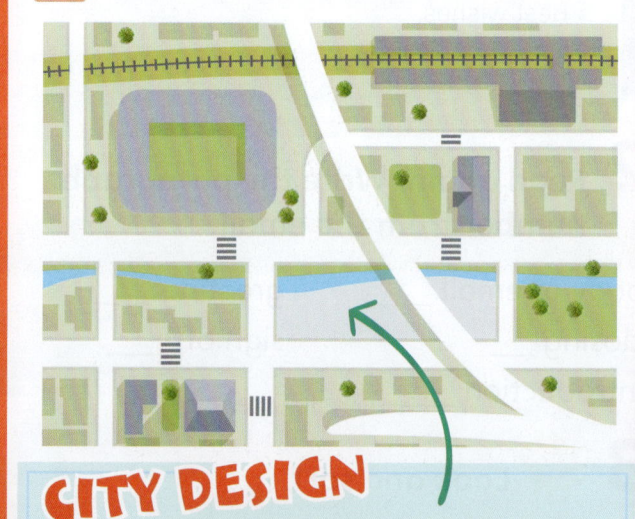

CITY DESIGN PROJECT COMPETITION!

What would you create in our city center project? Please present your plans and ideas at the city hall on June 19th at 10:00.

> I'd do a skyscraper with a living wall and solar panels.

> I'd create a park with lots of water features and an outdoor learning center.

132 one hundred and thirty-two

Step 3

Create

✈ Create your project.

- ☐ Create plans and drawings of your project.
- ☐ Think about who can help with your project. Architects? Gardeners? Engineers?
- ☐ Think about some materials you will need, like bricks, flowers, or water.

Step 4

Show and tell

✈ Present your project.

- ☐ Present your project to the class.
- ☐ Ask and answer questions about the projects.
- ☐ Have a class vote for the best project.

How would the project be ecological?

It would have solar panels and we'd plant lots of plants.

Where would the users of your skyscraper park their cars?

Complete the directions from the train station to the city hall.

Dear delegates

Thank you for agreeing to present your city project.

To get to the city hall from the train station _____

_____

_____

_____

Now I can …

- … use words to talk about places in a city.
- … use the second conditional.
- … ask for and give directions.
- … write instructions in an email.

one hundred and thirty-three 133

4 Checkpoint
UNITS 7 AND 8

1 🎧 070 Listen and complete the quiz for Vaun. Then find him in the picture in **2**.

FACING YOUR FEARS!
HOW DO YOU REACT TO CHALLENGES?

1 What's the scariest thing you've done?
- A I've walked through a dark tunnel with bats flying around.
- B I've slept outdoors under the stars.
- C I moved to a new city and started a new school.

2 Have you ever …
- A climbed to the top of a tall statue without looking down?
- B dived from a tall diving board?
- C held a scary spider in your hand?

3 Which situation have you experienced?
- A I've slept through my alarm and missed class.
- B I've got lost on an underground train network.
- C I've fallen over in front of people.

4 What would you do if you forgot your words in a presentation?
- A I'd run away and hide.
- B I'd start telling jokes.
- C I'd never forget my words. I'd always have notes with me.

5 Would you ever do a bungee jump off a skyscraper?
- A Only if someone else was with me.
- B Yes, I would. It sounds cool!
- C No way! I'm scared of heights.

6 Which of these makes you nervous?
- A I hate it when the lights go off in a storm. I'm scared of the dark.
- B I'm worried I might text the wrong person one day.
- C I'm scared of walking too close to a fountain. It might wet me!

NOW FIND OUT YOUR RESULTS!

Mostly As You prefer not to be in challenging situations. But when you are in a challenging situation, you are brave and determined.

Mostly Bs You are certainly not afraid of a challenge! Keep on having fun – but just be careful you don't put yourself in danger.

Mostly Cs You are right to think that danger isn't always fun! In your group of friends, you are probably the most sensible person. Your friends are lucky to have you around!

134 one hundred and thirty-four

CODE CRACKER

2 Read about Anya and Vaun's trip. What did each person experience?

Anya, Vaun, Juan, and Mona went hiking to a tower. They explored different places – a tunnel, a cave, a bridge, and the tower. In each place they had an unpleasant experience: someone fell over, heard a strange noise, felt something move, or saw spiders.

Clues
- Vaun heard a scary noise.
- The person who went into the tower heard a noise.
- Mona went into the cave.
- The person in the cave fell over.
- Anya didn't explore the bridge, the tower or the cave.
- The person in the tunnel felt something move.

	heard a noise	felt something move	saw spiders	fell over	tunnel	tower	bridge	cave
Anya								
Vaun	✓	✗	✗	✗	✗	✓	✗	✗
Juan								
Mona								

3 Write a dialog to continue the story. (Look back at page 117 for help.)
- What do the characters look like? Imagine their appearance.
- How do the characters speak?
- Where does the action happen?
- What sounds can you hear?

4 Look back at the quiz. Ask and answer with a partner. Find out how many of your classmates have the same results as you.

Test your progress with English Benchmark Young Learners

The United States of America
CULTURE

The United States of America

The United States of America (U.S.A.) is a country of 50 states covering a huge part of North America and including Alaska in the northwest and the islands of Hawaii. There is no official language of the U.S.A., but English is the main language and is used across the media, government, and, of course, in Hollywood. The capital city is Washington, D.C., but the largest city (and probably most famous) is New York.

Fun Fact!
The U.S. flag was designed by high school student Robert G. Heft as a school project and he only scored a B-! Robert's design was adopted as the new U.S. flag in 1960 and his teacher had to give him a higher grade!

1 071 Read and listen. Which cities are mentioned?

NEW YORK, NEW YORK
New York is famous for its stunning Manhattan skyline, the Statue of Liberty, and Central Park, the huge green space in the center of the city. The most famous skyscraper in New York is the Empire State Building. You can climb to the top and look out from the 102nd floor! If that doesn't scare you, a Frenchman once walked on a tightrope between two of the highest towers in New York!

HOORAY FOR HOLLYWOOD!
Everyone associates Los Angeles with Hollywood and the movie industry, with all the major movie studios based there. But L.A. also has many beautiful beaches. If you're not afraid of huge waves, you can surf at nearby Malibu beach.

WELCOME TO MIAMI
One city that can rival L.A. for beaches is Miami, Florida. You could even go swimming with sharks if you dared! Miami is a modern city with many skyscrapers. In fact, Miami has the third tallest skyline in the United States (after New York and Chicago).

OLDER AND WISER
St. Augustine, which like Miami is in Florida, is the oldest city in the United States. It was founded in 1565 and its oldest building was built in 1723. Another old building in St. Augustine is The Lightner Museum. It used to be a hotel called Hotel Alcazar. This beautiful building has twin bell towers and a courtyard with fountains and statues.

2 Read again and discuss.

1. If you could visit only one of the cities in the text, which would you visit? Why?
2. Which city in your country has the tallest buildings? Is the oldest? Is famous for its beach?

3 Create a city skyline silhouette.

4 Listen. Which national park is not mentioned? Check ✓.

a. Yellowstone National Park 
b. Everglades National Park 
c. Grand Canyon National Park 
d. Yosemite National Park

5 Listen again and check ✓.

Which national park …	Yellowstone	Everglades	Yosemite
1 has mountains?			
2 has black bears?			
3 has alligators and crocodiles?			
4 has a volcano?			
5 is subtropical?			
6 has grizzly bears?			

My Culture

6 Read and discuss.

1. What national parks are there in your country?
2. Have you ever visited a national park?
3. Why are national parks so important?

7 Research a national park in groups.

- Where is it?
- How big is it?
- What's the landscape like?
- What animals live there?

4 Food for the future!

LANGUAGE LAB: GRAMMAR 1: TALKING ABOUT THE FUTURE

5 Play *Future Game* in groups.

Start

- Your next meal
- Your next vacation
- After this class
- Plans for next weekend
- Predictions about yourself in 10 years
- The next movie you plan to see
- Transport in 2200
- Your breakfast tomorrow
- **Miss a go!**
- The environment in 2050
- After school today
- **Why ...?**
- Global temperatures in 2100
- Wildlife in the future
- New foods in the future
- Popular jobs in 2030
- The next thing you buy
- **How much/ many ...?**
- **Move back two!**
- Your family and friends in 2030
- **Where ...?**
- Your next sporting activity
- Your 18th birthday
- **What ...?**
- The next book you read
- **Go forward two!**
- The future of farming
- Your next trip to the supermarket
- Your hobbies in the future
- **How ...?**
- Next Saturday
- Your dinner this evening
- Your next trip to the beach
- The next popular singer or band
- Your next birthday party
- **Who ...?**
- The next clothes you plan to buy

Finish

138 one hundred and thirty-eight

Wordlist

Welcome Unit

School Day Vocabulary
assembly
bell rings
cafeteria
detention
gym
hallway
locker
lunch box
portable classroom
recess
schedule
stand in line
study hall

Unit 1

News Report Vocabulary
blog
caption
cyberbullying
headline
interview
news article
online
report
reporter
share
source
upload
vlog

Phonics
book
blog
bully
club
come
cushion
drum
foot
fun
good
lot
money
on
put
shop
son
sun
vlog
wash
watch

Experiment lab
boiling point
crash
dense
expand
freeze
freezing point
gas
hexagonal
ice
liquid
molecule
snowflake
solid
steam

Unit 2

Adjectives to Describe People
brave
compassionate
determined
generous
inspirational
intelligent

Inspirational Jobs Vocabulary
author
campaigner
charity worker
lawyer
researcher
volunteer

Phonics
beach
bead
bread
breakfast
clean
dream
eat
feathers
head
healthy
heavy
pea
read
sea
tea
team
wealthy
weather

one hundred and thirty-nine 139

Wordlist

Experiment lab
antibiotic medicine
bacteria
microscope
mold
particles

Culture lab
achievement
climate change
dynamite
Europe
moose
Nobel Prize
Stockholm
Sweden
United Nations

Unit 3

Business Vocabulary
advertisement
cash
earn
price
product
save
sell
spend

Phonics
blow
blue
boat
few
floats
gold
interview
new
shoes
yellow

Experiment lab
bracelet
invent
kit
loom band
loss
profit
rubber band
weave

Unit 4

Food Vocabulary
carbohydrate
dairy
fat
fiber
minerals
protein
vitamins

Farming Vocabulary
agriculture
intensive farming
organic farming
pesticides
pollinators
sustainable farming

Phonics
August
blue
caught
drew
flew
flute
June
saw
thought
true

Experiment lab
carnivore
ecosystem
food chain
herbivore
omnivore
primary consumer
producer
quaternary consumer
secondary consumer
tertiary consumer
vegan
vegetarian

Culture lab
agriculture
crafts
Fair Trade
jewelry
Kenya
Nairobi
profitable
recycled
sustainable
traditional
tribes
waste

Unit 5

Ancient Egypt Vocabulary
archeologist
burial place
coffin
dig
hieroglyphics
hole
mummy
papyrus
pyramid
treasure

Phonics
bear
burn
curtain
fur
hurt
pear
share
somewhere
there
wear
where
word
work

Experiment lab
blocks
force
friction
logs
ramp
ropes
sled
stone

Unit 6

Airports and Travel Vocabulary
arrivals
baggage
check-in
departure gate
emigrating
land
language exchange
passport
security
take off
terminal

Phonics
fire
flowers
hire
hour
our
tire
tower

Experiment lab
biometrics
chip
database
fingerprint
information
iris
recognition
scan
voice

Culture lab
British
hieroglyphics
London
Rosetta Stone
the United Kingdom
transport
treasures
underground

Unit 7

Situations to Avoid Vocabulary
called your teacher "Mom" by mistake
dropped your phone
forgotten your words on stage
got lost in a maze
looked down from the top of a skyscraper
overslept and missed the start of class
slept alone in the dark
slipped on a banana skin
texted the wrong person
turned off the internet

Phonics
answered
bright
climbing
frightened
heights
knife
knot
know
neighbor
night
thumb
wrap
wrist
written
wrong
wrote

Wordlist

Experiment lab
afraid
beat
digestive system
fear
fight
flight
heart
lungs
pupils
sweat

Experiment lab
fountain
jet
pool
pump
tranquil
water feature
waterfall

Culture lab
alligators
American
bears
crocodiles
Los Angeles
Miami
national park
New York
skyline
St. Augustine
the U.S.A.

Unit 8

My City Vocabulary
city hall
crosswalk
factory
office building
overpass
sidewalk
skyscraper
stadium
statue
tunnel
university

Continents
Africa
Antarctica
Asia
Australia
Europe
North America
South America

Phonics
a
an
elegant
European
hospital
hour
office building
one-way
underground train
university

Grammar Reference
LEVEL 5 REVISION

Unit 1

Grammar 1
Must/Mustn't for obligation:

I *must* do my homework.
You *mustn't* be late.

Grammar 2
Have to for obligation (affirmatives/negatives/questions):

You *have to* wear funny clothes and masks.
She *doesn't have to* play music.
Do you *have to* learn to juggle? No, you don't.

Unit 2

Grammar 1
Simple Past with Wh- questions and irregular verbs:

Object Questions:
Where did you go last Saturday?
Subject Questions:
Who went with you?

Grammar 2
Simple Past questions with *what/which* + noun:

What food *did* you eat?
We ate cake in the cafe.

Which activity *did* you like best?
I liked playing sports.

Unit 3

Grammar 1
Present Progressive for future plans (affirmatives/negatives/questions):

Tomorrow, *we're going* on holiday.
Is Mom relaxing tomorrow? Yes, she is.

Grammar 2
Phrases to talk about time:

I'm eating lunch *at noon*.
He's leaving *at midnight*.

one hundred and forty-three

Grammar Reference
LEVEL 5 REVISION

Unit 4

Grammar 1
Comparative and superlative adjectives:

Panda Party is *funnier than* Ancient Times.
Paint With Me is *more colorful than* The Old House.
The Old House is *as frightening as* Tiger Trouble.
My Desert Holiday is *the most interesting* book.
Panda Party is *the best* book ever!

Grammar 2
***Might* for future possibilities:**

I *might* read Tiger Trouble next weekend.
My brother *might not* enjoy The Old House.
She *might* go to the bookstore after school.
We *might not* find an interesting book in the library.

Unit 5

Grammar 1
Present Perfect to talk about experiences (affirmatives/negatives/questions):

I *have been* to a theme park.
I *haven't eaten* cotton candy.
I *have never been* on a Ferris wheel.
Has she ever hiked up a mountain? No, she hasn't.

Grammar 2
Interrogatives with *how*:

How high is the Ferris wheel?
It's 80 meters high.

How fast is the rollercoaster?
It's 78 km per hour.

How long does it take to get to the theme park?
It takes half an hour.

How much does it cost?
It costs $25.

Unit 6

Grammar 1

Wh- questions using the Simple Past and Past Progressive:

What were you doing when you *found* the secret waterfall?
I *was exploring* the jungle when I *found* the secret waterfall.

Grammar 2

Certainty and uncertainty:

It *must be* hot because it is very sunny.

It *might/could be* cold because it is raining.

It *can't be* warm because it is snowing.

Unit 7

Grammar 1

Present Passive (affirmatives/questions):

Soccer *is played* in lots of countries across the world.

What *are* soccer balls *made* from?
Soccer balls *are made* from a type of plastic.

Is food *sold* at soccer games?
Yes, food *is sold* at soccer games.

Grammar 2

Count and uncount nouns with *too much/ too many/enough/not enough*:

I have *too much* pasta.
He has *too many* shoes.
They have *enough* balls.
She doesn't have *enough* water.

Unit 8

Grammar 1

Tag questions (positive/negative):

You like dancing, *don't you*?
We can play, *can't we*?
You're not tired, *are you*?

Grammar 2

Adjectives with *-ing* and *-ed* endings (describing objects/feelings):

A competition? That sounds *exciting*.
I feel *excited*.
That looks *tiring*. I feel *tired*!

one hundred and forty-five 145

Grammar Reference

Unit 1

Grammar 1

Reported speech (statements):

"I *ride* my bike to school."
He said that he *rode* his bike to school.

"We always *walk* to school."
They said that they always *walked* to school.

"I *take* the subway. I *don't want* to be late."
She said that she *took* the subway. She *didn't want* to be late.

"They *go* to school by car."
She said that they *went* to school by car.

Grammar 2

Reported speech (questions):

"*Do you like* walking to school?"
She asked them *if they liked* walking to school.

"*What time do you take* the subway?"
They asked her *what time she took* the subway.

"*What do you do* after school?"
I asked him *what he did* after school.

"*When do you get* home from school?"
She asked him *when he got* home from school.

Unit 2

Grammar 1

Relative clauses (*which*, *who*, *where*, *when*, *whose*, *that*):

He's the reporter *who* interviews famous actors.
This is the article *that* he wrote.
This is *where* his online articles are uploaded.
That was the evening *when* he met the movie director.
He's the reporter *whose* article won a competition.
Here's the interview *which* I read last week. It's very funny!

Grammar 2

Used to (affirmatives/negatives/questions):

I *used to* read his movie reviews every week.
I *didn't use to* watch his vlog.
He *didn't use to* interview actors. He *used to* take photos.
My parents *used to* buy a newspaper every day. They *didn't use to* read the news online.

Did people *use to* share news articles online? No, they didn't.

Did she *use to* upload photos to her blog? Yes, she did.

Grammar Reference

Unit 3

Grammar 1

Modals for obligation and advice (*have to/don't have to/must/mustn't/should/shouldn't*):

You *should* stand in line outside the classroom.
You *shouldn't* talk when the teacher is talking.
You *mustn't* eat in the library.
They *must* take the test next week.
You *have to* walk in the hallway.
He *has to* go to the principal's office!
They *don't have to* go to assembly today.
She *doesn't have to* go to detention.

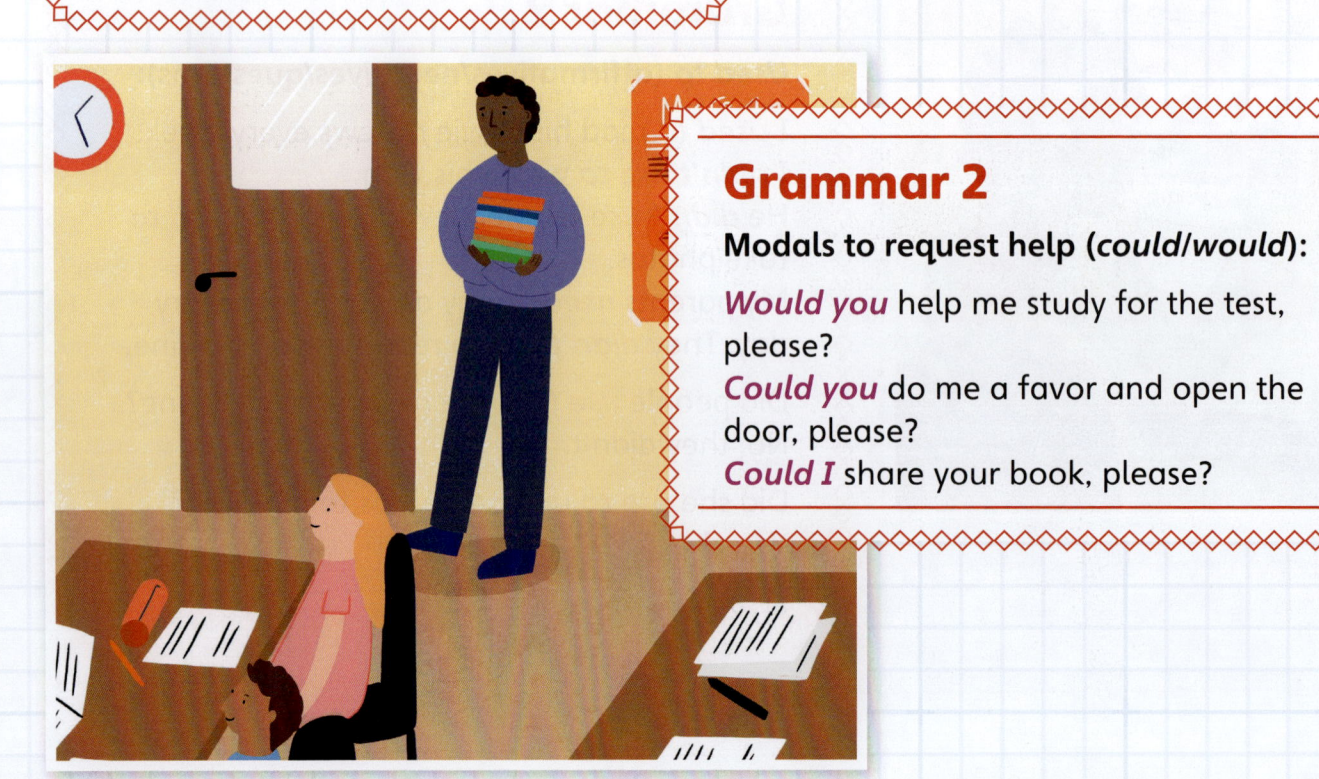

Grammar 2

Modals to request help (*could/would*):

Would you help me study for the test, please?
Could you do me a favor and open the door, please?
Could I share your book, please?

Unit 4

Grammar 1

Future using *will*, *going to* and the Present Progressive:

We *will* go to Japan in the future.
It *won't* be too expensive.
I'm *going to* eat sushi.
I'm buying a guidebook tomorrow.

Do you know where you *will* stay?
We *will* stay in a hotel.

Are you *going to* see any cherry blossom?
Yes, I hope so.

Grammar 2

Might and will for future possibilities and certainties:

The weather *might* be sunny in Japan. It's spring.
We *might* hike up a mountain.
We *might not* go shopping every day.
It *will* be busy in Tokyo. It's a big city.
We *will* visit a palace. It's in a beautiful park.
We *won't* speak Japanese.

Grammar Reference

Unit 5

Grammar 1

Past Passive (affirmatives/negatives):

The product *was invented* three years ago.
It *was designed* by a conservationist. He wanted his invention to be good for the environment.
It *wasn't sold* in stores. It *was sold* online.
The profits *weren't spent* by the inventor.
They *were given* to charity.
The shoes *were talked about* in an article online.

Grammar 2

Past Passive (questions):

Where *was* the product *invented*?
It *was invented* in Sweden.

When *was* the advertisement *made*?
It *was made* two years ago.

What *were* the shoes *made* from?
They *were made* from recycled materials.

Why *were* the shoes *wanted* by everyone?
Because they *were worn* by a famous basketball player.

Were the shoes *sold* in lots of countries?
Yes, they were.

Unit 6

Grammar 1

Present Perfect Progressive with *for* and *since*:

Have you *been waiting* here *for* long?
I've *been waiting* for you *since* ten o'clock!

She's *been studying for* two hours.

He *hasn't been reading* that book *for* long.

What have they *been doing since* school finished?
They've *been doing* their homework *for* half an hour.

Grammar 2

Present Perfect with *just*, *already*, *yet* and *still*:

Have you chosen a book *yet*?
Yes, *I've already found* an interesting book. It's about endangered animals.

He still hasn't finished reading that book about ancient rome. He needs more time.
We've just seen a movie about pyramids.

Have they finished their homework *yet*?
No, they haven't.

Grammar Reference

Unit 7

Grammar 1

Present Perfect and Simple Past:

Have you ever cooked lunch for your family?
Yes, I have.

When *did* you *cook* lunch?
I cooked lunch for my family last week.

Have you and your parents ever eaten vegan food?
Yes, we have!

What *did* you *eat*?
We ate vegan burgers. I often make them for my family.

Grammar 2

**Presentation skills:
Tips on how to plan your presentation**

- Write brief notes to remind you of the key points.
- Use short, simple sentences.
- Speak clearly and loudly.
- Practice your presentation in front of other people if you can.
- Make eye contact with the people you're talking to.
- End the presentation with a conclusion or summary.

Unit 8

Grammar 1

Second Conditional:

If I were older, *I'd travel* to lots of countries.
If we had more money, *we'd stay* in expensive hotels.
He'd do a language exchange *if he had* more time.
They wouldn't go camping *if they didn't have* a caravan.
If they lived nearer to the airport, *would they go* abroad more often?

Grammar 2

Prepositions of movement (*across, along, past, over, around, through*):

How do we get to the departure gate? We've walked *around* the airport for ages!

First, go *over* the bridge to get to the other terminal.
Then you need to go *past* check-in.
You have to go *through* security.
Walk straight *across* the hall.
Then go *along* the hallway to the departure gate.

Irregular verbs

	Simple Present	Simple Past	Present Perfect
be	I am You are He/She/It is We are They are	I was You were He/She/It was We were They were	I have been You have been He/She/It has been We have been They have been
be able to	I can You can He/She/It can We can They can	I could You could He/She/It could We could They could	
build	I build You build He/She/It builds We build They build	I built You built He/She/It built We built They built	I have built You have built He/She/It has built We have built They have built
buy	I buy You buy He/She/It buys We buy They buy	I bought You bought He/She/It bought We bought They bought	I have bought You have bought He/She/It has bought We have bought They have bought
do	I do You do He/She/It does We do They do	I did You did He/She/It did We did They did	I have done You have done He/She/It has done We have done They have done
eat	I eat You eat He/She/It eats We eat They eat	I ate You ate He/She/It ate We ate They ate	I have eaten You have eaten He/She/It has eaten We have eaten They have eaten
find	I find You find He/She/It finds We find They find	I found You found He/She/It found We found They found	I have found You have found He/She/It has found We have found They have found

	Simple Present	Simple Past	Present Perfect
fly	I fly You fly He/She/It flies We fly They fly	I flew You flew He/She/It flew We flew They flew	I have flown You have flown He/She/It has flown We have flown They have flown
get	I get You get He/She/It gets We get They get	I got You got He/She/It got We got They got	I have gotten You have gotten He/She/It has gotten We have gotten They have gotten
give	I give You give He/She/It gives We give They give	I gave You gave He/She/It gave We gave They gave	I have given You have given He/She/It has given We have given They have given
go	I go You go He/She/It goes We go They go	I went You went He/She/It went We went They went	I have gone You have gone He/She/It has gone We have gone They have gone
grow	I grow You grow He/She/It grows We grow They grow	I grew You grew He/She/It grew We grew They grew	I have grown You have grown He/She/It has grown We have grown They have grown
have	I have You have He/She/It has We have They have	I had You had He/She/It had We had They had	I have You have He/She/It has We have They have
know	I know You know He/She/It knows We know They know	I knew You knew He/She/It knew We knew They knew	I have known You have known He/She/It has known We have known They have known

Irregular verbs

	Simple Present	Simple Past	Present Perfect
lose	I lose You lose He/She/It loses We lose They lose	I lost You lost He/She/It lost We lost They lost	I have lost You have lost He/She/It has lost We have lost They have lost
make	I make You make He/She/It makes We make They make	I made You made He/She/It made We made They made	I have made You have made He/She/It has made We have made They have made
meet	I meet You meet He/She/It meets We meet They meet	I met You met He/She/It met We met They met	I have met You have met He/She/It has met We have met They have met
read	I read You read He/She/It reads We read They read	I read You read He/She/It read We read They read	I have read You have read He/She/It has read We have read They have read
run	I run You run He/She/It runs We run They run	I ran You ran He/She/It ran We ran They ran	I have run You have run He/She/It has run We have run They have run
say	I say You say He/She/It says We say They say	I said You said He/She/It said We said They said	I have said You have said He/She/It has said We have said They have said
see	I see You see He/She/It sees We see They see	I saw You saw He/She/It saw We saw They saw	I have seen You have seen He/She/It has seen We have seen They have seen

	Simple Present	Simple Past	Present Perfect
speak	I speak You speak He/She/It speaks We speak They speak	I spoke You spoke He/She/It spoke We spoke They spoke	I have spoken You have spoken He/She/It has spoken We have spoken They have spoken
stand	I stand You stand He/She/It stands We stand They stand	I stood You stood He/She/It stood We stood They stood	I have stood You have stood He/She/It has stood We have stood They have stood
take	I take You take He/She/It takes We take They take	I took You took He/She/It took We took They took	I have taken You have taken He/She/It has taken We have taken They have taken
tell	I tell You tell He/She/It tells We tell They tell	I told You told He/She/It told We told They told	I have told You have told He/She/It has told We have told They have told
throw	I throw You throw He/She/It throws We throw They throw	I threw You threw He/She/It threw We threw They threw	I have thrown You have thrown He/She/It has thrown We have thrown They have thrown
wear	I wear You wear He/She/It wears We wear They wear	I wore You wore He/She/It wore We wore They wore	I have worn You have worn He/She/It has worn We have worn They have worn
write	I write You write He/She/It writes We write They write	I wrote You wrote He/She/It wrote We wrote They wrote	I have written You have written He/She/It has written We have written They have written

OUR WORLD

INTRO:
Here we stand: children of every age,
This is our world and the world's our stage.
We can laugh, we can cry – we can float, we can fly,
We can dance, we can sing – we can do almost anything
in OUR world ... our *beautiful* world.

VERSE 1:
Some of us are small; some of us are tall,
Some of us are shy; some of us say hi to everybody,
Some of us like numbers; some of us love words,
Some of us watch football, and some of us watch the birds!

(CHORUS)
This is *our* world ... we're different but the same.
We live and learn together – we get to know each other ...
in OUR world ... our *beautiful* world.

VERSE 2:
Some of us like music; some of us like cars,
Some of us draw pictures, looking at the stars,
Some of us are scientists, trying to find the code,
All of us can help a friend and give a hand to hold.

This is *our* world – there's room for everyone.
We learn to live together, and we have a lot of fun ...
In *our* world ... in *our* world ... in our beautiful world!

English Code

Level 6

CERTIFICATE

_____

WELL DONE!

Student's Name

Teacher's Signature and Date

Now I can ...

Stickers